Computer Modeling and Simulation Reference Text

Stanislaw Raczynski

Computer Modeling and Simulation Reference Text

Stanislaw Raczynski
Universidad Panamericana.
Facultad de Ingeniería.
Augusto Rodin 498, Ciudad de México, 03920, México.

Academica Press
Washington

Library of Congress Cataloging-in-Publication Data
Names: Raczynski, Stanislaw (author)
Title: Computer modeling and simulation : reference text | Raczynski, Stanislaw
Description: Washington : Academica Press, 2025. | Includes references.
Identifiers: LCCN 2025945995 | ISBN 9781680533835 (hardcover) |
9781680533842 (e-book)

Contents

Preface

This text should be treated as an auxiliary source of information and reference about modeling and simulation. You can quickly search for specific topics using the table of contents or using the index. Some topics are very short, and some are more detailed, extending to several pages. In most of the topics the literature references are given inside the text or at the end of the corresponding topic section. Figure and equation numbers, if any, start from one within each section. In the e-book version, inside the text, there are clickable links that help you consult other topics, if necessary.

See the section "What simulation is?" for some definitions of *simulation*.

Chapter 1

Modeling and Simulation: General Concepts

What Simulation is?

There are many definitions of computer simulation. For example, Alan B. Pritsker defines it as *the representation of the dynamic behavior of the system by moving it from state to state in accordance with well-defined operating rules* (Pritsker, Introduction to Simulation and SLAM II, John Wiley and Sons, 1984). Many authors define simulation in a similar way, with emphasis to the changes of the modeled system state in time.

Bernard P. Zeigler in *Theory of Modeling and Simulation,* John Wiley and Sons, 1976 writes: *We can therefore define simulation as the technique of solving problems by the observation of the performance, over the time, of a dynamic model of the system.* In somewhat more general way, we can define the modeling as the relation between real systems and models, and *simulation* as the relation between models and computers.

In the article of A.A.B. Pritsker, *Compilation of definitions of simulation,* SIMULATION, August 1979, pp.61-63, you can find about 30 different definitions of computer simulation. Most of the authors tend to define simulation in terms of the software they develop or use. However, the common approach is that of relating simulation with the changes of the model state in time.

Ralph Huntsinger, past president of the Society for Computer Simulation was always saying that simulation is fun. This is true, taking into account the interdisciplinary aspect of computer simulation. A specialist in simulation must learn how aircraft fly, how the rice grows, how shoes are produced, how an epidemics spreads, how a legal process works, how galaxies are formed among other things. This is the FUN you find dealing with computer simulation.

Ethics Code

This code is adopted by the following organizations:
SCS http://www.scs.org/- Society for Modeling and Simulation International (Resolution http://www.sisostds.org/webletter/siso/iss_98/art_557.htm)
MISS - Mcleod Institute of Simulation Sciences (Resolution http://www.site.uottawa.ca/~oren/SCS_MISS/MISS-PaP.pdf)
M&SNet http://www.site.uottawa.ca/~oren/SCS_MSNet/MSNet-index.htm - McLeod Modeling and Simulation Network (Resolution http://www.site.uottawa.ca/~oren/SCS_MSNet/MSNet-PaP.htm)
SISO http://www.sisostds.org/ - Simulation Interoperability Standards Organization (Resolution http://confs.itcenter.org/listprocedu/ViewMessage.cfm?Client=SISO&Message_ID=76284&Reflector_ID=202&WhereStmt=10%2F08%2F03&OrderStmt=Date%5FSubmitted%20DESC%2C%20Time%5FSubmitted%20DESC&UseMostRecentMessages=False)
SISO Canada http://www.drdc-rddc.dnd.ca/seco/societies_e.html (Resolution http://www.sisostds.org/sisocanada/)

Preamble

Simulationists are professionals involved in one or more of the following areas:

1. Modeling and simulation activities.
2. Providing modeling and simulation products.
3. Providing modeling and simulation services.

Personal Development and Profession

As a simulationist I will:

1. Acquire and maintain professional competence and attitude.
2. Treat fairly employees, clients, users, colleagues, and employers.
3. Encourage and support new entrants to the profession.
4. Support fellow practitioners and members of other professions who are engaged in modeling and simulation.
5. Assist colleagues to achieve reliable results.
6. Promote the reliable and credible use of modeling and simulation.

7. Promote the modeling and simulation profession; e.g., advance public knowledge and appreciation of modeling and simulation and clarify and counter false or misleading statements.

Professional Competence

As a simulationist I will:

1. Assure product and/or service quality by the use of proper methodologies and technologies.
2. Seek, utilize, and provide critical professional review.
3. Recommend and stipulate proper and achievable goals for any project.
4. Document simulation studies and/or systems comprehensibly and accurately to authorized parties.
5. Provide full disclosure of system design assumptions and known limitations and problems to authorized parties.
6. Be explicit and unequivocal about the conditions of applicability of specific models and associated simulation results.
7. Caution against acceptance of modeling and simulation results when there is insufficient evidence of thorough validation and verification.
8. Assure thorough and unbiased interpretations and evaluations of the results of modeling and simulation studies.

Trustworthiness

As a simulationist I will:

1. Be honest about any circumstances that might lead to conflict of interest.
2. Honor contracts, agreements, and assigned responsibilities and accountabilities.
3. Help develop an organizational environment that is supportive of ethical behavior.
4. Support studies which will not harm humans (current and future generations) as well as environment.

Property Rights and Due Credit

As a simulationist I will:

1. Give full acknowledgement to the contributions of others.

2. Give proper credit for intellectual property.

3. Honor property rights including copyrights and patents.

4. Honor privacy rights of individuals and organizations as well as confidentiality of the relevant data and knowledge.

Compliance with the Code

As a simulationist I will:

1. Adhere to this code and encourage other simulationists to adhere to it.

2. Treat violations of this code as inconsistent with being a simulationist.

3. Seek advice from professional colleagues when faced with an ethical dilemma in modeling and simulation activities.

4. Advise any professional society which supports this code of desirable updates

The System

Modeling and simulation (M&S) concepts almost always refer to the notion of *system*. By a *system*, we mean a *set of components that are interrelated and interact with each other*. These interrelations and interactions differentiate the system from its environment. The system is supposed to be organized in order to perform one or more functions or *achieve one or more specific goals*. McNamara in his book (McNamara, C., (2006) Field Guide to Consulting and Organizational Development, Authenticity Consulting, LLC, ISBN-10 1933719206.) defines a system as follows: "*... a system is an organized collection of parts (or subsystems) that are highly integrated to accomplish an overall goal. The system has various inputs, which go through certain processes to produce certain outputs, which together, accomplish the overall desired goal for the system.*" The commonly mentioned properties of systems include:

Aggregation—that means that systems can be grouped into categories that can be nested into larger aggregates.

Non-linearity—System needs not be linear, i.e., it does not necessarily satisfy the principle of superposition.

The **behavior of a system** is not the sum of the behaviors of its components.

In this text, by ***Dynamic System*** we mean a system which state and other descriptive variables change in time according to well-defined rules of interaction.

Consult: Holland, J. H. (1995) Hidden order. Addison-Wesley

System state

Consider a dynamic system with an input and output signals U and Y, respectively. We define by $X(t)$ the *state of the system* at the moment t if and only if a function or functional F exists such that

$X(t) = F(t, U\{s, t\}, s, X(s)), s < t$.

Here, $U\{s,t\}$ is the system input over the interval $[s,t]$. In other words, it is necessary that the system state at a moment t can be calculated using some past state in time instant s and the input function over the interval between the two moments of time. For example, the state of a system that has one spring, one mass and one damper linked together is given by the mass position and velocity. All the other descriptive variables of this system are parameters, inputs (e.g. external forces), or some output functions defined by the modeler.

Causal System

First, define what the phrase "*equivalent functions*" means. Obviously, two functions equal to each other in all points of the given interval are equivalent to each other. For a system with input and output signals, we treat two input signals as equivalent, if they produce the same output. For example, if the system is an integrator, two input signals that are equal to each other on $[t_o,t_1]$, except a set of points of total measure zero are equivalent. Other example is a sampled data system (e.g. a digital controller with an A/D converter at the input) with sampling period T. Two different input signals that coincide only at $t=0,T,2T,3T....$ are equivalent to each other because the system cannot observe the values in time instants other than the sampling moments.

Consider a dynamic system which state is defined as X. Suppose that we can define an input and output signals for this system as U and Y, respectively. The system is said to be *causal* if and only if for every t_1

$U_1(t)$ equivalent to $U_2(t)$ over an interval $[t_o,t_1]$, implies that $Y_1(t_1)$ = $Y_2(t_1)$

where $Y_1(t_1)$ and $Y_2(t_1)$ are two outputs at the time instant $t = t_1$, obtained with inputs U_1 and U_2, respectively, and t_o is a fixed initial time instant, $X(t_o)$ fixed. The output signal is supposed to be an algebraic function of the system state. We suppose that the system state at t_o is the same for the two possible trajectories.

An example of a non-causal system is

$$Y(t) = \int_{-\infty}^{\infty} p(t-s)U(s)\,ds$$

where $p(t)$ is a function different from zero everywhere. In this case, the value of Y at the time instant t depends not only on the past, but also on the future values of the time. If we replace p by the Dirac impulse at zero, then the system becomes causal (in this case simply $Y(t) = U(t)$).

Classification of Dynamic Systems

- Finite automata
- Infinite automata
- Systems with concentrated parameters
- Systems with distributed parameters
- (Systems described by algebraic equations are not dynamic systems)

This classification of dynamic systems frequently appears in books on the dynamics of physical systems and control systems. It may be useful while looking for a software for a particular simulation task. The first two groups (Finite and infinite automata) can be simulated with discrete event simulation, and the other need continuous simulation tools.

Below are given short characteristics of the four classes of dynamic systems. Note that the word “automata” does not mean a robot or automatic manipulator. This is a term used in the early works on information theory and cybernetics.

Finite automata – finite number of possible states. For example, a light switch, a computer. Modeling tool: discrete events.

Infinite automata – infinite, but enumerable set of possible states. For example, a waiting line without limit, infinitely growing population. Modeling and simulation tool: discrete events Chapter 4.

Concentrated parameter systems – for this class, the power of the set of all possible states is equal to the power of the set of the real numbers. For example, RC circuit, a mass moved by a spring and a dumper. Main modeling tool: ODE (Ordinary Differential Equations).

Distributed parameter systems – the power of the set of all possible states is greater than the power of the set of all reals. For example: diffusion process, 3D heat distribution in a piece of metal, waves on the water surface. Main modeling tool: PDE (Partial Differential Equations).

Collaborative simulation modelling (CSM)

This term was introduced by the GROUPSIM Network (www.groupsim.com) to refer to the many possible forms of human and computer collaboration that exist in simulation modelling.

Research topics focus on the support of human-to-human (H2H) interaction (computer supported cooperative work/groupware and simulation) and support of computer-to-computer (C2C) interaction (distributed simulation, parallel and distributed simulation, and web-based simulation), and the synergies between the two.

There are other approaches to collaborative simulation. Complex engineering systems (such as aerospace vehicle, locomotive, automobile, robot, etc.) are usually integrated with multi-subsystems in physical domain such as mechanical multi-body system, electronic system, hydraulic servo system, and control system. The design and development of such a complex engineering system need naturally multidisciplinary collaboration. Furthermore, multidisciplinary model-couple issue and its collaborative simulation are identified and crucial in this research as the major characteristics to bring dynamism to collaborative design. To make the analysis of complex product more accurate in the systematic level is the objective in the research of collaboration design.

Consult: Zhang H M. A solution of multidisciplinary collaborative simulation for complex engineering systems in a distributed heterogeneous environment. Sci China Ser F-Inf Sci, 2009, 52(10): 1848-1862, doi: 10.1007/sll432-009-0153-2

Experiment planning

The design of experiments refers to the process of planning of experiments in a way that appropriate data can be analyzed through statistical methods, resulting in valid and objective conclusions. Before we can run a simulation program and analyze the output, we need to choose a simulation model and decide which outputs to collect. To head in the right direction, we should have some well-defined goals and questions when we start, but we should expect to develop new goals and questions as we go along.

The benefits of the design of experiments in simulation include the possibility of improving the performance on the simulation process, avoiding the trial-and-error techniques to seek solutions.

Passive data collection leads to a number of problems in statistical modeling. Observed changes in a response variable may be correlated with, but not caused by, observed changes in individual factors (process variables). Simultaneous changes in multiple factors may produce interactions that are difficult to separate into individual effects. Observations may be dependent, while a model of the data considers them to be independent.

Designed experiments address these problems. In a designed experiment, the data-producing process is actively manipulated to improve the quality of information and to eliminate redundant data. A common goal of all experimental designs is to collect data as parsimoniously as possible while providing sufficient information to accurately estimate model parameters.

Full factorial designs measure response variables using every treatment (combination of the factor levels). A full factorial design for n factors with $N_1, ..., N_n$ levels requires $N_1 \times ... \times N_n$ experimental runs-one for each treatment. While advantageous for separating individual effects, full factorial designs can make large demands on data collection.

How should they be varied? Use the same or different random numbers across configurations?

Run length?

Number of runs?

Interpretation, analysis of output?

How to make runs most efficiently?

Probability distributions:

In stochastic simulation, outputs are observations from (unknown) probability distributions

Ideally, estimate the whole distribution -ambitious goal usually get summary measures of output distributions

Means (maybe too much focus on these)

Variance, standard deviation

Response Surfaces

Response surface methodology (RSM) explores the relationships between several explanatory variables and one or more response variables. The method was introduced by G. E. P. Box and K. B. Wilson in 1951. The main idea of RSM is to use a sequence of designed experiments to obtain an optimal response.

Most experimental designs are based on an algebraic regression model, where

Output = dependent (Y) variable

Inputs = independent (x) variables

For more detail consult the references below Books:

Design and analysis of simulation experiments Serge? Mikha?lovich Ermakov,Vi?a?cheslav Borisovich Melas

Design and Analysis of Simulation Experiments Series: International Series in Operations Research & Management Science , Vol. 111 Kleijnen, Jack P.C. 2008, XIV, 218 p. 26 illus., Hardcover ISBN: 978-0-387-71812-5

David J. McArthur , Philip Klahr , Sanjai Narian, ROSS: an object-oriented language for constructing simulations, Expert systems techniques, tools and applications, Addison-Wesley Longman Publishing Co., Inc., Boston, MA, 1986

David J. McArthur , Philip Klahr , Sanjai Narian, ROSS: an object-oriented language for constructing simulations, Expert systems techniques, tools and applications, Addison-Wesley Longman Publishing Co., Inc., Boston, MA, 1986

Articles:

Box, G. E. P. and Wilson, K.B. (1951) On the Experimental Attainment of Optimum Conditions (with discussion). Journal of the Royal Statistical Society Series B 13(1):1–45.

Etherington, D.W., A. Borgida, R.J. Brachman, and H. Kautz. (1989). Vivid Knowledge and Tractable Reasoning: Preliminary Report. Proceedings of the Eleventh International Joint Conference on Artificial Intelligence. IJCAI-89.

Fikes, R.E. and N.J. Nilsson. (1971). STRIPS: A New Approach to the Application of Theorem Proving to Problem Solving. Proceedings of the Second International Joint Conference on Artificial Intelligence. IJCAI-7 I.

Fox, M.S. and Y.V. Reddy. (1982). Knowledge Representation in Organization Modeling and Simulation: Definition and Interpretation. Proceedings of the Thirteenth Annual Pittsburgh Conference on Modeling and Simulation. University of Pittsburgh, School of Engineering, Volume 13.

Fox, M.S. and K. Sycara. (1990). Overview of CORTES: A Constraint Based Approach to Production Planning, Scheduling and Control. Proceedings of the Fourth International Conference on Expert Systems in Production and Operations Management. ESPOM-90.

Fox, M.S. and K. Sycara. (1991). CORTES Project 1991 Annual Report. In preparation.

Frederking, R.E. and L.L. Chase. (1990). Planning in a CIM Environment: Research Towards a Constraint-DirecteM Planner. Proceedings of the Fourth International Conference on Expert Systems in Production and Operations Management. ESPOM-90.

Hayes-Roth, B., F. Hayes-Roth, S. Rosenchein, and S. Cammarata. (1979). Modeling Planning as an Incremental, Opportunistic Process. Proceedings of the Sixth International Joint Conference on Artificial Intelligence. IJCAI-79.

H J Levesque, Making believers out of computers, Artificial Intelligence, v.30 n.1, p.81-108, Oct. 1986 [doi>10.1016/0004-3702(86)90068-8]

Reddy, Y.V. and M.S. Fox. (1982). Knowledge Representation in Organization Modeling and Simulation: A Detailed Example. Proceedings of the Thirteenth Annual Pittsburgh Conference on Modeling and Simulation. University of Pittsburgh, School of Engineering, Volume 13.

Stephen D. Roberts, Joe Heim, A prespective on object-oriented simulation, Proceedings of the 20th conference on Winter simulation, p.277-281, December 12-14, 1988, San Diego, California, United States [doi>10.1145/318123.318202]

Steven F. Roth, Joe Mattis, Data characterization for intelligent graphics presentation, Proceedings of the SIGCHI conference on Human factors in computing systems: Empowering people, p.193-200, April 01-05, 1990, Seattle, Washington, United States [doi>10.1145/97243.97273]

Sacerdoti, E.D. (1973). Planning in a Hierarchy of Abstraction Spaces. Advance Papers of lJCAi-73. IJCAI-73.

Sacerdoti, E.D. (1975). The Nonlinear Nature of Plans. Advance Papers of lJCA1-75. IJCAI-75.

Sathi, N., M.S. Fox, V. Baskaran, J. Bouer. (1986). S imulationCraftTM: An Artificial Intelligence Approach to the Simulation Life Cycle. Proceedings of SCS Summer ,Simulation Conference. Reno, Nevada.

Sathi, A., M.S. Fox, and M. Greenberg. (1985). Representation of Activity Knowledge for Project Management. IEEE Transactions on Pattern Analysis and Machine Intelligence, PAMI-7,5, 531-551.

Veloso, M.M. (1989). Nonlinear problem solving using intelligent casual-commitment Technical Report. School of Computer Science, Carnegie Mellon University.

David E. Wilkins, Practical planning: extending the classical AI planning paradigm, Morgan Kaufmann Publishers Inc., San Francisco, CA, 1988

Modeling and Simulation, descriptive variables

In general, we can define the *modeling* as the relation between real systems and models, and *simulation* as the relation between models and computers.

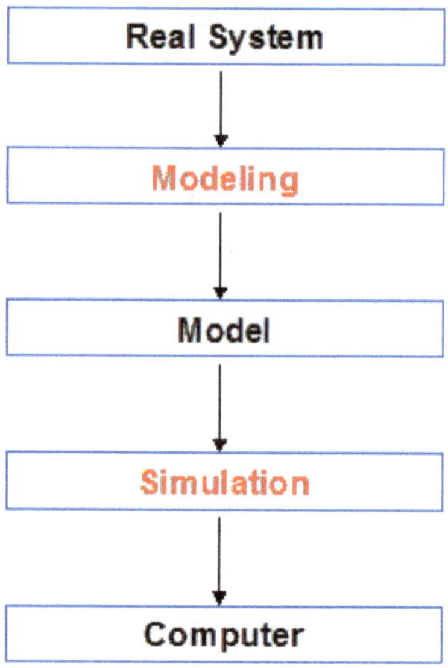

Modeling and simulation

P. Bratley, L.F. Bennet and L.E.Schrage in their book *A guide to Simulation*, Springer-Verlag, 1987, say: A model is a description of some system intended to predict what happens if certain actions are taken. This is perhaps one of the most essential definitions of what a model of a real system is, although it needs some additional explications. Many years ago A.Rosenblueth and N.Wiener pointed out that modeling is one of the central needs of scientific reasoning. Dealing with models we must take into account many factors like the level of simplification, experimental frame, model validity, tractability, credibility and the aim of modeling among others. Bernard P. Zeigler (*Theory of Modeling and Simulation*, John Wiley and Sons, 1976) gives some basic concepts on modeling.

First of all, we must define the *model components* as elemental parts of the model, like clients in a bank, ships entering a harbor, cars on a street, etc. Each component is described by the *descriptive variables* that include input, state and output variables. The set of all descriptive variables in a model is the *experimental frame* of the model. The same real system may have several different experimental frames. For example, a possible experimental frame for a model of an electronic circuit may include currents and voltages in all circuit elements. Other experimental frame may include the temperatures of all elements (ICs, resistors, etc.) and the temperature distribution in the printed circuit. Obviously, the two experimental frames lead to different models and satisfy different modeling purposes. Each experimental frame results in the corresponding simplified model, as shown on the following figure.

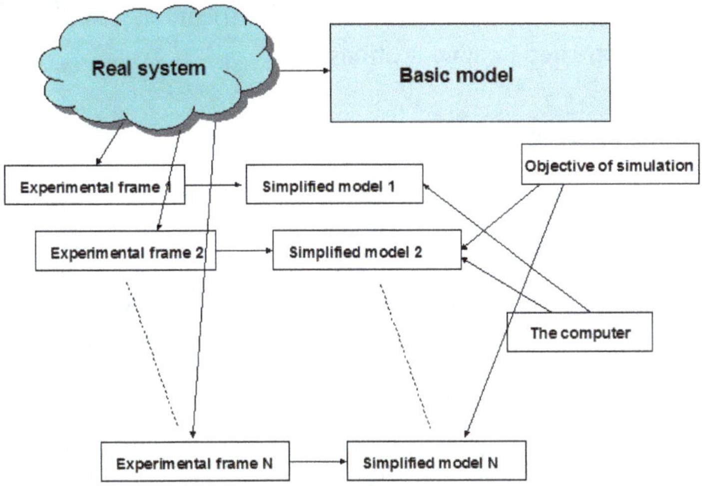

Basic model, experimental frames and simplified models.

Here, the ***basic model*** is that which reflects exactly the behavior of the real system. Such model normally does not exist.

Note that the aim of the modeling task, as well as the technical limitations (the computer on which we want to run the resulting simulation program) reduce the number of possible simplified models. This helps us select the appropriate simplification. If there is more than one simplification that satisfies these criteria, we must apply other selection rules (e.g. modeling cost). If no model exists that satisfies our aim and technical limitation, then no modeling is possible. Remember that looking for something that does not exist is simply a waste of time.

There are many types of models, used in model classification. The model can be:

ICONIC - when represents reality on a smaller scale,

ANALOG or DESCRIPTIVE - shows reality in maps, charts and diagrams,

SYMBOLIC - uses mathematical expressions to portray reality,

PREDICTIVE - used in predictive analytics to create a statistical model of future behavior,

NORMATIVE - evaluates alternative solutions to answer the question, "What is going on?" and suggests what ought to be done or how things should work according to an assumption or standard.

The concepts of model validity, verification, credibility and tractability are treated in other sections.

Object- and Agent-based modeling

Recall that in the *object-oriented (OO) programming* the program is composed by objects. An *object* is a structure that has its *attributes* (visible from outside of the object or hidden) and *methods*. Everything the object "knows" is in its attributes and everything it can do is in its methods. For example, a particle, which is a component of an N-body system, has a set of attributes that include its position and velocity vectors, its mass, shape, dimensions etc. The methods of the particle should describe the way it interacts with other particles (calculate the external forces) and the particle movement. The difference between OO programming languages and OO simulation tools is that an OO **simulation language or package must provide the clock mechanism**, transparent for the user. For example, Simula 67 is an object-oriented programming language. Its simulation mechanisms are not in the language definition, but rather in a pre-defined PROCESS class, written in Simula. It can be used to create other objects. The PROCESS class handles the model time and the event queue. Other examples of OO simulation are MODSIM III and BLUESSS.

The advantage of OO simulation consists in more realistic model building. For example, the classical prey-predator models were formulated in the form of Lotka-Volterra differential equations. However, the Lotka-Volterra equations does not exactly describe what really happens in the real prey-predator systems. Simulating such systems with object-oriented tools we describe the behavior or each of its members, taking into account its position in a geographical region, individual attributes, etc. This results in more realistic simulations

This approach consists in describing individuals interacting with one another and with their environment. The individuals may be of different types. Although the rules for behavior are shared by a group of individuals of the same type, the behavior is not identical for all of them. This modeling method has many applications, mainly in ecology, biology and social sciences. The ecologist can take into account individual and local variability, and study its relation to macroscopic (population-community-level) system behavior. The implementation of such models leads to the discrete-event simulation and object-oriented programming (Huston M., DeAngelis D. and Post W., *New computer models unify ecological theory.* BioScience, 38(10), pp. 682-691). See also Lotka-Volterra equation.

Agent-based modeling is a similar approach. However, instead of simple individuals the main components of the model are *agents* that are supposed to behave according to somewhat more complicated rules. Agents can have their aims, beliefs, artificial intelligence, and the capability to negotiate.

Agents are autonomous problem-solving entities that can interact with others and respond to changing circumstances.

Literature:

EPSTEIN, M.E. and Axtell, R. 1996. *Growing Artificial Societies - Social Science from the Bottom Up.*Washington: Brookings Institution Press. Cambridge, MA: MIT Press.

GESSLER, N. 1997, Growing Artificial Societies - Social Science from the Bottom Up. *Artificial Life* 3: 237-42.

KIRMAN, A. 1992. Whom or What Does the Representative Agent Represent. *Journal of Economic Perspectives* 6: 126-39.

MINAR, M., Burkhart, R., Langton, C., Askenazy, M. 1996, *The Swarm Simulation System: A Toolkit for Building Multi-agent Simulations*. Santa Fe Institute.

RUSSELL, S.J and Norvig, P. 1995. *Artificial Intelligence - A Modern Approach.* Upper Saddle River: Prentice Hall.

See also: SWARM:

Metamodeling

The term *metamodeling* is used to emphasize the we are abstracting and describing the thought process which lie behind developing specific models of specified systems. Thus, we are concerned to abstract the essentials of modeling and move attention away from the details toward the essentials of the system in general. This concept mainly refers to the theory and applications of the bong graphs method to simulate physical systems.

Consult: Karnopp D.C., Rosenberg R.C., *System dynamics: A unified approach,* John Wiley, 1990.

Linear Dynamic Systems

Consider a dynamic system S with well-defined inputs and outputs. The system is said to be *linear* if and only if it satisfies the principles of superposition and homogeneity. The principle of superposition is satisfied when the response to excitations $x_1,x_2,x_3,\ldots,x_N$ applied simultaneously, is the sum of responses $y_1,y_2,y_3,\ldots,y_N$, where y_k is the response to x_k. This must be satisfied for any combination of values of the excitation variables. The principle of homogeneity is satisfied when the response to ax is equal to ay, y being the response to x and a is a constant.

Note that due to this definition, the function $y = ax + b$, a and b constant, is not linear. However, such (afine) functions can be easily linearized, simply changing the notation: If $z = y - b$ then after substituting $y = z + b$ to the original equation, we obtain a function which is linear with respect to z.

A differential equation $dx/dt = f(x, dx/dt,t)$ is linear, when the function f is linear with respect to x and its derivative (not necessarily with respect to the independent variable t). This applies also when x and f are vectors.

A system, which input-output relations and described by linear functions is linear. In particular, if a system is described by a linear differential equation, then it is said to be linear.

See also: Transfer function and State transition matrix

Model Validation

Model *validity* is one of the central problems in modeling and simulation. Consider a real, dynamic system and its model. Let ***S*** be the operation of modeling (passing from real system to the model). By ***X(t)*** we will denote the system state in the time instant ***t*** , by **y(t)** the system output, by *f* the state transition function that maps the state ***X(t)*** and input over **[*t*, *t*+*h*]** into the new state ***X(t+h)***. The same letters with suffix **s** denote the corresponding items for the model. Our model is said to be valid if and only if the following diagram commutes.

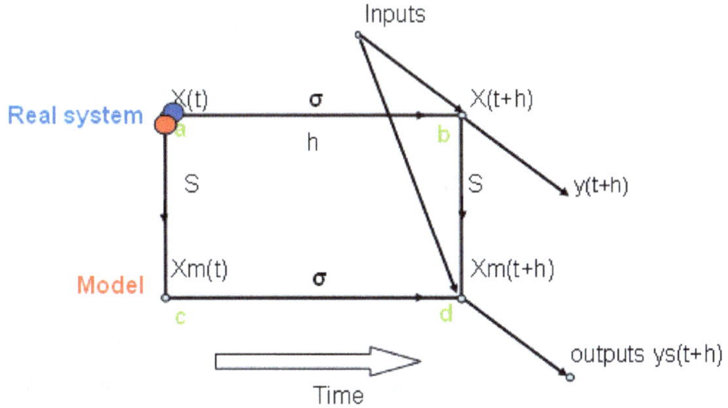

Validation due to Zeigler: The model is valid if the above diagra commutes.

X – the state of the real system, Xm model state, S – Operation of modeling, σ – state transition function

Validation due to Bernard Zeigler.

In other words, starting with ***X(t)*** we must obtain the same model output $y_s(t+h)$ independently of the way we go. This must be satisfied for **any** possible initial state and input.

The above definition of model validity is somewhat difficult for practical applications. A more practical concept is the "*input-output*" *validity* that can be illustrated by the following scheme.

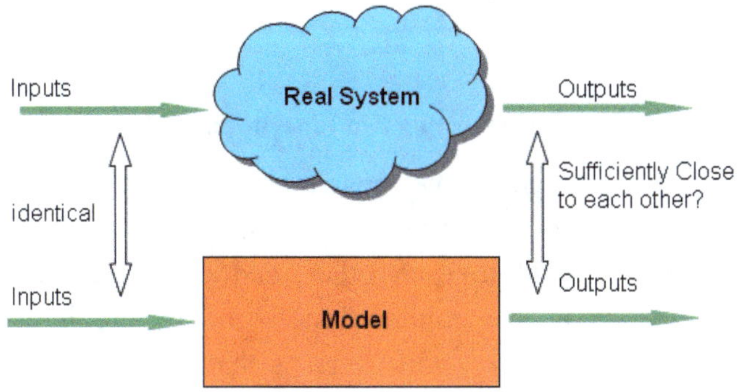

This validation needs data about the system behavior in the past

Input-output validation.

The model is supposed to be *I/O valid*, if the outputs from the model and from the real system are "sufficiently" near. What "sufficiently" means is the individual judgment of the modeler. Obviously, the above property must be satisfied for a long time interval, and perhaps for future model inputs. As we do not know what inputs signals will affect our model, the only way to check the I/O validity is to compare the model behavior and the real system output using some historic data.

Observe that according to the first definition, **any approximation of a real and continuous system by a model with discrete time is invalid.** Indeed, in a real system a disturbance may come within the time period of discretization, being not detected by the discrete model. If the input signals have high frequencies, the aliasing phenomenon may result in completely wrong results. Another source of error is the time-discretization itself that implies its own errors. The most direct way to make the discrete model more exact is to decrease the sampling time for the discrete model. However, there are limitations for such approach, mainly caused by the computer resolution and limitations of a numerical method applied for trajectory integration. Anyway, the modeler must look for a reasonable compromise.

Invalid models are often results of wrong assumptions. Creating a simplified model, we idealize the real system that may result in physically wrong models. Consider a simple example of the following electric circuit.

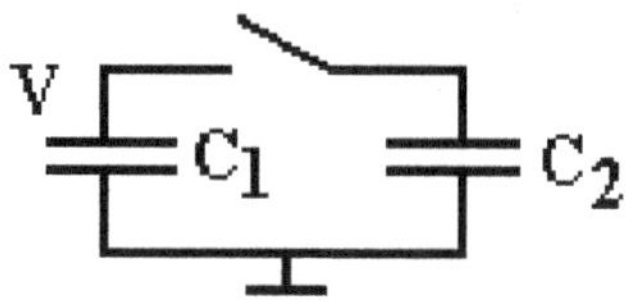

Connecting two capacitors.

Let the initial voltage for the capacitor $\mathbf{C_1}$ be equal to **V**, and initial voltage for $\mathbf{C_2}$ equal to zero. After closing the switch, the two voltages become obviously equal to each other, and equal to **V/2**, provided $\mathbf{C_1=C_2=C}$. Now, consider a simplified model of the circuit. We assume that all elements are "ideal," which means that the capacitors have no internal resistance or inductance, the same assumption taken for the conductors (**R=0**). Now calculate the initial energy of the circuit. It is equal to **$(CV^2)/2$** . After closing the circuit, the total energy is **$2(C(V/2)(V/2))/2$** = **$(CV^2)/4$**. Where the half of the initial energy went? Our model cannot explain this. In other words, **the model is invalid**. The very simple reason is that it is too simplified. Now, consider other model, where the connecting wires have resistance **R**. It is easy to show that the half of the energy is dissipated in the wire resistance during the transient process. Moreover, that this energy **does not depend** on the value **R** of the resistance. This means that the previous simplified model is not the limit case of the second model, with **R** approaching zero.

Note also that the model validity depends on the actual experimental frame. The first model of our circuit is valid if the experimental frame only includes the (static) voltages. However, if we add the system energy to the experimental frame, this model becomes invalid and we must look for other one (**R**>0).

Model Credibility

A model is credible if the user believes that it is valid and useful. This means that a model can be valid and not credible. Also, a credible model can be invalid. The best way to create credible models is to involve the future user in the process of model development.

Simulation program verification

Program verification must be done to check that the simulation program operates in the way that the model implementer thinks it does; the program must be free of bugs and consistent with the model. Such checking is never absolutely complete. The program testing problem is a complex one and widely treated in data processing systems, but the problems are similar. Good verification makes the simulation model and program more believable to the user.

Variance reduction

Frequently, we seek to estimate some measure of performance using some statistics over the resulting sets of values, mostly the mean value. Variance reduction techniques try to reduce the true variance of such statistics. It should be noted that this attempts not always are conceptually correct. First, the mean we obtain is not the most important result, and sometimes it may be confusing and provide little information. Second, reducing variance is changing the model statistical properties, and this makes the model validity questionable. In other words, if the real system reveals big variance, the model should behave in similar way and any variance reducing operations simply make it invalid. However, in some situations (e.g. Monte-Carlo integrations and simulation) these methods may be useful.

Let X and Y are the random outputs of two simulations driven by pseudo random number streams U and V , respectively. Note that Var[X+-Y] = Var[X] + Var[Y] + 2Cov[X,Y]. From this equality some important properties of the variance are derived that give rise to the following variance reduction techniques.

* Common random numbers. Compare policies corresponding to X and Y respectively, using X - Y as an estimator of E[X - Y].

* Control variates. For a fixed policy, let X be a principal output, and Y a control variate with E[Y] = 0. Use X - kY as an estimator for E[X].

* Antithetic variates. For a fixed policy, let X be the output of run number one, and Y the same output for run two. Use (X + Y)/2 as an estimator for E[X].

For a detailed discussion of these techniques consult:

P.Bratley, B.L. Fox and L.E.Schrage, A guide to simulation, Springer-Verlag, 1987.

Qualitative modeling and reasoning

These terms have become widely discussed topics in the recent artificial intelligence (AI) literature [1] and [2] below. The *qualitative simulation* [3] includes a capability of creating lumped models through model simplification, relaxation of system variables, and a tendency toward topological, graph-based methods for high-level modeling of systems. The *process abstraction* and *model evolution* are important features of qualitative simulation. This permits the researchers to specify incomplete or fuzzy models and view qualitative reports, and then to use new modeling and simulation tools that contain capabilities of specifying model at different levels of abstraction.

For example, a real, physical system like an electronic RLC circuit or a pendulum with uncertainty can be viewed from a qualitative point of view. If we are uncertain about possible external excitations, we might abstract the model behavior by lumping, using intervals, or using fuzzy mappings from linguistic features like “growing” or “oscillating” to real vector space.

The term *reasoning* means the act of starting with several knows and deriving an unknown (performed recursively).

Qualitative reasoning consists in producing a process model that uses symbolic and intuitive knowledge. This suggests a comprehensible and “commonsense” approach to modeling and simulation. The qualitative reasoning methodology is closely related to the main concepts of *cognitive science*.

The nature of *cognition* includes thinking, learning, problem solving, language and its interactions with conceptual structure, and other aspects of mental life. It embodies a convergence of cognitive psychology with computer science, developmental studies, and work in linguistics, artificial intelligence, anthropology, neuroscience, and philosophy. What brings these disciplines together, is the central tenet that a broad range of mental processes are computational in nature and that these processes operate on mental representations. Sometimes the implementations of these ideas to computer simulation is called *cognitive simulation.*

However, we should be careful while using intuition and the “commonsense” approach mentioned earlier. The common sense, emphasized in some methodologies, like the theory of restrictions is not always the best way of scientific thinking. Note that the most important discoveries in the history of humanity originated with ideas that were apparently in conflict with the common sense (in the time they were proposed): How crazy and obviously out-of-common-sense was the idea of Copernicus that the earth moves around the sun!

Even more contradictory to the common sense was the Einstein’s conclusion, telling that the mass is equivalent to energy.

Going back to computer simulation it should be noted that both qualitative reasoning and simulation might provide new methods and tools. Up to now, the qualitative simulation is rather the question of results interpretation and experiment planning.

References

[1] Bobrow D.G., Qualitative reasoning about physical systems, MIT Press, 1985.
[2] Kuipers B., Artificial intelligence, 29(3), pp.298-338, September 1986.
[3] Cellier F., Qualitative simulation of technical systems using the general system problem solving framework, International Journal of General Systems, 13(4), pp. 333-344, 1987.

Soft Systems

Soft Systems Methodology (SSM) was developed in early 1980s by Checkland and Wilson. The aim of SSM is an alternative to the traditional "hard" or deterministic approaches. SSM is being applied mainly to systems that include human behavior. The model components used in SSM are:

Owners that monitor the model and take appropriate control actions
Actors - the running model components
Customers - the beneficiaries or victims of the system
The World View - the perspective taken in defining the system
Transformations - the rules of interaction and input-output relations

Soft systems are mostly systems that involve human, ecological or biological factors that hardly can be described using deterministic models. The examples can be found in social sciences, simulation of political and economic systems and in models that involve human decision making. The simplest, but rather primitive way to simulate soft systems is what frequently is called system dynamics. The tools of system dynamics played significant role in modeling and simulation. While simulating social systems, it is important to understand the system structure and its internal interactions rather than to produce exact projections of systems trajectories. Such modeling effort can be useful in other "dimension" of modeling. A good example of this is a model of the Shakespeare's Hamlet presented on one of the System Dynamics conferences (*Implementation of Stella to illustrate Hamlet,* Pamela Lee Hopkins, Desert View High School, Tucson Arizona, 1984 System Dynamics Conference). The model is designed to expose the effect of some events have on Hamlet's willingness to kill Claudius. This permits the examination of the impact of each event as it occurs and as Hamlet continues to contemplate the situation. The model variables are, among others the motivation to avenge, new evidence, old evidence, motivation per death, aging, opportunity to act, etc. Obviously, the author's objective was not to repeat the sequence of events of the original Hamlet, or to write new Shakespeare-style dramas. As stated in the article, *the model forces the students to sequence events, thereby improving their understanding of the dramatic action of the play. The model provides a meaningful language, in the form of numbers, for students to discuss psychological concepts, emotions, and the resulting behaviors. This promotes student involvement in discussion of the difficult concepts of a critically acclaimed piece of literature.*

Consult

Checkland P.B., 1981, Systems Thinking, Systems Practice. Chichester: Wiley.

Wilson B., 1984, Systems: Concepts, Methodologies and Applications. Chichester: Wiley.

Computational Tractability

It is well known in the operations research that some problems that have a nice mathematical description cannot be solved using the hardware we actually have. The same occurs with models prepared to be run on a computer as a simulation task. Some models are **computationally intractable,** which means that they are too time-consuming or expensive to be realized.

A modeling and simulation task is *intractable* if its computational complexity increases exponentially with the number of its descriptive variables. The **computational complexity** can roughly be defined as the minimal cost of guaranteeing that the computed answer to our question (simulation task) is below the required error threshold.

A mostly cited example of an intractable problem is the *salesman problem*, namely the simulation of all possible routes of a salesman that must visit various cities. The aim of such simulation is to find the route with shortest distance possible. Other examples in continuous system simulation can be found in fluids dynamics applied to problems like reentry of space shuttle to the atmosphere of the earth (modeling the airflow around the craft).

For more discussion on intractability consult Joseph F. Traub and Henryk Wozniakowski, *Braking intractability,* Scientific American, January 1994, or Arthur G. Werschulz, *The computational complexity of differential and integral equations: An information-based approach,* Oxford University Press, 1991.

Uncertainty

Static case and general remarks

By *static case* we mean models that does not involve differential equations. In section II of this topic the dynamic case is considered.

The data obtained as a result of observations or measurements from a real, physical system provide only a mapping of the reality to some abstract model parameter set. Any measurement or data estimation is somewhat uncertain. Recall that the famous *uncertainty principle* of Heisenberg pointed out that it is impossible to measure both the position and the momentum of a particle (e.g. electron, neutron) accurately at the same time. Moreover, there is an absolute limit of the product of the accuracy of these two parameters, having as the lower limit *h/2pi*, h being the *Plank's constant*. We will not discuss this principle here because it belongs to quantum physics rather than modeling. The only conclusion we should remember is that no absolutely exact measurements exist, even in the theory.

According to academic definitions given in various encyclopedia we can see that *uncertain* means *not certainly known, questionable, problematical, not reliable, vague, not definite, vague, doubtful, not having certain knowledge, not sure, occurring by chance, ambiguous.*

Frequently, uncertainty is understood in terms of probability. The value of a realization of a random variable is uncertain. What we may be given is some information about the probabilistic properties of the variable, like its probability density function or variance. However, uncertainty not always can be defined in terms of probability. There are situations where the probability distribution is unknown or does not exist at all. In many cases the probability is not relevant. If you will be operated for appendicitis, the information that in hospital A the probability that you die is equal to 0,0003 and in hospital B it is equal to 0,0005 is not very important. You just have two options: go to hospital A or B, and you will decide using other criteria. You will be operated only once, and the information that you probably survive 1999 operations out of 2000 is somewhat abstract to you.

Due to A. Bargiela (*Uncertainty - a key to better understanding of systems*, Keynote Lecture, Proc. 10th European Simulation Symposium, pp.11-29), uncertainty in systems modeling has the following contexts or "dimensions."

* Entropy
* Confusion
* Dissonance
* Nonspecifity
* Vagueness

Perhaps the most popular measure of uncertainty is entropy. However that it can be only used when the uncertainty is expressed in terms of probability. **Entropy** is the scientific term for the degree of randomness or disorder in processes and systems.

It was first defined by the German physicist Rudolf Clausius in 1865, based in part on earlier work by Sadi Carnot and Lord Kelvin. The concept of entropy plays an important part in the modern discipline of information theory, in which it denotes the tendency of communications to become confused by noise or static. The American mathematician Claude E. Shannon first used the term for this purpose in 1948.

Confusion can be defined as the belief associated with sets of information that are not entirely enclosed within the body of evidence or are in real or potential conflict with the body of evidence.

Dissonance is the plausibility associated with sets of information that are not intersecting with the body of evidence or are conflict with the body of evidence.

Non-specificity and **Vagueness** are more subjective attributes of a model (in fact, defines in somewhat *vague* way). They appear while modeling soft systems described with fuzzy logic or systems with uncertain structure. Also, the (human) decision making processes frequently lead to such models.

There are several methods for uncertainty treating. In the static case, with no system dynamics involved, the problem is to estimate the intervals of the system state variables, using the information provided as a set of measurements. Let x be the system state. The set of measurements is a mapping from the system state space to the measurement space given by the formula $z = g(x)$, z being a measurement value. The mapping g is not exactly known and in most cases it is non-linear. We are given a set Z of measurement results, and we pretend to find the corresponding set X of system states. The dimensions of this set are the *confidence intervals* for the components of the system state. **Do not confuse these intervals with the confidence interval obtained by probabilistic methods**.

The most frequently used methods in uncertainty analysis are:

* Monte Carlo method
* Linear programming
* Sensitivity analysis (sensitivity matrix)
* Ellipsoid method

All these methods are used to find the inverse of the mapping g. For more detail consult (Boris T. Polyak a, Sergey A. Nazin a, Cécile Durieu b, Eric Walter c Ellipsoidal parameter or state estimation under model uncertaintyAutomatica, Volume 40, Issue 7, July 2004, Pages 1171-1179).

Uncertainty in continuous dynamic system modeling.

Models are frequently charged with some *uncertainty*. This may be caused by the errors in parameter estimation, or by the influence of the external, constant, or fluctuating control signals and disturbances. A common approach to uncertainty treatment is the use of random variables. This is also referred to, as *stochastic models* that include such variables in the equations of model dynamics. However, observe that, to use random variables, we must know their probabilistic properties, like the expected value, variance, probability distribution, and others. These data may be difficult to obtain in practical applications. Instead, it is probable that we only know the limits where the variable can change. In this case, the statistical methods can hardly be applied or may provide wrong results. The point is that an *uncertain variable* need not be a *random variable*. The uncertainty may cause fluctuation, permanent constant changes, or unpredictable tendencies. For example, this may be caused by natural disasters, or an erroneous information generated intentionally, like in the stock market models (remember also the law of Murphy).

Such uncertain factors are called *tychastic variables*, as defined in Aubin JP, Saint-Pierre P (2005) A tychastic approach to guaranteed pricing and management of portfolios under transaction constraints. See "Random Fields and Applications," Centro Stefano Franscini, Ascona. In: Seminar on Stochastic Analysis, Random Fields and Applications V. https://doi.org/10.1007/978-3-7643-8458-6_22.

The *reachable sets* may show the influence of such uncertain variables on the system behavior. Note that using tychastic variables, the *problem statement is deterministic*. We define the restrictions for *tychastic* variables and then calculate the shape of the reachable set of the model affected by them. This gives us insight into possible model uncertainty in the form of the RS.

Consult sections "Differential inclusions and reachable sets" and "Stock Market Simulation" for more comments on uncertainty treatment.

Neural Networks

Neural networks in computer simulation are artificial imitations of biological neural nets that appear in living organisms, in particular in the human brain.

The principal component of such systems is a *neuron* cell. It has a central star like bulb, called the *soma* that contains the nucleus of the cell. Stretching out of the soma at one end is a long nerve fiber, called *axon* that can be several centimeters long. Along the axon the cell's output signal is transmitted. Spouting off from the axon may be many smaller branches, bifurcating a number of times. At the end of each of these is to be found a little *synaptic knob* (nerve ending). At the other end of the soma and often branching out in all directions from it, are the tree-like *dendrites.* The dendrites carry the neuron input signals to the soma.

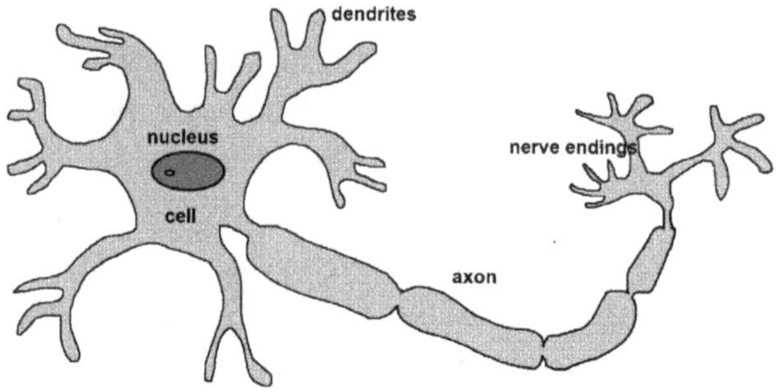

The signals pass from one neuron to another through the junctions known as *synapse* where a synaptic knob of one neuron is attached to a soma or a dendrite of the other neuron. A nerve fiber consists of a cylindrical tube containing a mixed solution of salt and potassium chloride. The chloride ions are present inside and outside the tube in different proportions, so there is a negative electric charge inside the tube. A signal along the fiber consists of a region in which this charge imbalance is reversed, moving along the fiber. To produce a signal, the neuron must *fire.* This event depends on a complicated non-linear function of the signals it receives. Some neurons have synaptic knobs, which emit a neurotransmitter chemical with a tendency to "encourage" the soma of the next neuron to fire. These synapses are called *excitatory.* Others tend to discourage the soma of the next neuron from firing and are called *inhibitory.* The total effect of the excitatory synapses which are active at the moment is added up, and the effect of the inhibitory ones is subtracted from this. If the result reaches certain critical threshold, the neuron is induced to fire (produce an impulse signal).

In computer models of neural networks or artificial neural networks the neurons are modeled as two-state components that can change the state between passive to firing. All inputs from the other neurons have assigned numerical values (weights) that multiply the effect of incoming signals. A non-linear function of the neuron makes the neuron fire. Computer neural networks do not follow rigidly programmed rules. Rather, they build an information base through a trial-and-error method. A programmer, for instance, will digitally input a photographic image for a neural network to identify, and it will "guess" which circuits to "fire" (activate) to identify the photograph and output the correct answer. Pathways between individual circuits are "strengthened" when a task is performed correctly and "weakened" if performed incorrectly. In this way a neural network "learns" from its mistakes and gives more accurate output with each repetition of a task.

Simple neural networks were built in the late 1950s, but little progress was made in the field until more powerful parallel processing techniques were developed a few decades later. Current neural networks are still far simpler than the human brain that has more than 100 billion neurons. By the 1990s computer software simulating neural networks had reached the market and was being used for such tasks as optical character recognition, credit risk assessment, and financial forecasting. Neural networks are well suited for artificial intelligence research, particularly in the areas of pattern recognition and voice recognition.

DESIRE is an interactive simulation optimization, combines neural networks (up to 20,000 connections), dynamic systems (to 2,000 differential equations) and graphics.

Platform: PC or SPARC station

Contact: G.A and T.M. Korn Industrial Consultants, RRI Box 96C, Chelan, WA 98816

This is a part of MATLAB system. This part of MATLAB is used to simulate neural networks. The Neural Network Toolbox is a comprehensive environment for neural network research, design, and simulation. As they require intensive matrix computations, MATLAB provides a natural framework for rapidly implementing neural networks and for studying their behavior and application. The Neural Network Toolbox provides comprehensive support for the design, implementation, and simulation of many proven network paradigms and is completely extensible. Its consistent methodology and modular organization facilitate research, provide a flexible framework for experimentation, and simplify customization. Contact: The Math Works, Inc., 24 Prime Park Way,

Natick, MA 01760.

References

Bullock, T. H., *Introduction to Nervous Systems* (1977); Chalmers, N., et al., eds.

Anderson, J., *An Introduction to Neural Networks* (1995); Caudill, M., In Our Image: Building an Artificial Person (1993).

Inverse mechanics

Generally speaking, inverse problems are concerned with the determination of the inputs and the characteristics of a system, given certain aspects of its output. Mathematically, such problems are ill-posed and have to be overcome through development of new computational schemes, regularization techniques, objective functionals, and experimental procedures.

Modeling and simulation can help in many mechanical and general engineering and bio-medical inverse problems. Perhaps the most important fields are robotics and human body modeling. For example, an important problem in robotics is to find the force that produce a particular motion and not vice versa. This is used to determine the control signals for the robot.

Examples of disciplines that need to solve inverse problems include

Seismic and medical imaging, seismic inversion

Non-destructive material characterization, and structural health monitoring

Inverse scattering

Bio-medical imaging and tissue characterization

Ground-penetrating radar imaging

Inverse problems in heat transfer

Damage characterization

Optimal design of experiments

Parameter identification

Real-time model updating

Consult

Inverse Problems in Engineering Mechanics

International Symposium on Inverse Problems in Engineering Mechanics 1998 (ISIP '98) Nagano, Japan

Edited by: M. Tanaka and G.S. Dulikravich

ISBN: 978-0-08-043319-6

Monte Carlo simulation

In the field of numerical methods, Monte Carlo method is applied mainly to evaluate integrals. For example, given a function f(x) with values in [0,1] and defined over the interval [0,1] the Monte Carlo method consists in randomly generating a set of points (x,y) in the square area 1x1 and in counting the points for which y<f(x). I f the number of such points is N and the total number of points is M, then the integral of f(x) over the given interval can be approximated by N/M. There are methods to make this procedure more effective, mainly by the reduction of the variance of the Monte Carlo result. In computer simulation we frequently deal with models that include some random parameters, variables or external excitations. In such simulation the resulting system trajectory is a random function, different for each simulation run. Taking some statistics over the resulting values is a Monte Carlo evaluation of the result.

Monte Carlo simulation is a method for iterative evaluating a model using sets of random numbers as inputs. This method is often used when the model is complex, nonlinear, or involves more than just a couple uncertain parameters. A simulation can typically involve over 10,000 evaluations of the model, a task which in the past was only practical using super computers.

Monte Carlo simulation has been widely used to simple problems like stock management and simple queuing models.

See also: CristalBall. and @RISK.

Cellular simulation

In this kind of modeling and simulation, we consider a n-dimensional region, where a grid of cells is defined. Each cell has its state that can change over time t. Normally, the time t is discrete and advances with step 1. The state of the cell may change according to its previous state, the state of cells from the cell neighborhood, and the rules of interaction. The cellular simulation was introduced in the 1940s by Stanislaw Ulam and John von Neumann. Norbert Wiener and Arturo Rosenblueth developed a model of excitable media with some of the characteristics of a cellular automaton.

The cellular simulation results in moving patterns that resemble living organisms. It may also generate interesting patterns and fractals. There are also applications of this type of simulation in games.

Cellular models are also referred to as cellular spaces, tessellation automata, homogeneous structures, cellular structures, tessellation structures, and iterative arrays

Virtual Reality

Virtual Reality (VR) is a useful graphical support for computer simulation. Though VR itself is not simulation, its graphical capabilities can help in the result representation, training, etc.

VR is a computer-generated environment with and within which people can interact. VR encompasses a range of interactive computer environments, from text-oriented on-line forums and multiplayer games to complex simulations that combine audio, video, animation, or three-dimensional graphics; and scent. Some of the more realistic effects are achieved using a helmetlike apparatus with tiny computer screens, one in front of each eye and each giving a slightly different view so as to mimic stereoscopic vision. Sensors attached to the participant (e.g., gloves, bodysuit, footwear) pass on his or her movements to the computer, which changes the graphics accordingly, to give the participant the feeling of movement through the scene. Computer-generated physical feedback adds a feel to the visual illusion, and computer-controlled sounds and odors reinforce the virtual environment. Other VR systems, such as FLIGHT SIMULATORS, use larger displays and enclosed environments to create an illusion. Less complicated systems for PERSONAL COMPUTERS manipulate an image of three-dimensional space on a computer screen. VR is used in some ELECTRONIC GAMES, in amusement-park attractions, and to simulate construction designs. Experimental and envisioned uses include education, industrial design, surgical training, marketing and art.

WRL is an ISO/IEC language developed by a combined effort of a group of companies and 3D designers and programmers for describing 3D scenes on the Web. The documents have *. WRL extensions that can be viewed by a browser with an appropriate plugin or helper-application.

This language is gaining more and more acceptance as a technology for displaying 3D graphics because it's a simple and accessible way to create interactive worlds. Also, an important feature is that VRML is encoded in UTF-8 (Unikey) format, similar to your web page's HTML encoded in ASCII, so you can make very detailed 3D scenes using very small files that can be downloaded quickly - which is one of the main concerns when putting something on the internet. For example: you can make a 3D animation logo embedded on your home page that takes much less time to be downloaded than usual animated gif.

Simulation interoperability standards

The Simulation Interoperability Standards Organization (SISO) is an international organization dedicated to the promotion of modeling and simulation interoperability and reuse for the benefit of a broad range of M&S communities. SISO's Conference Committee organizes Simulation Interoperability Workshops (SIWs) in the US and Europe. SISO's Standards Activity Committee develops and supports simulation interoperability standards, both independently and in conjunction with other organizations. SISO is recognized as a Standards Development Organization (SDO) by NATO and as a Standards Sponsor by IEEE. In addition, SISO is a Category C Liaison Organization with ISO/IEC (JTC 1) for the development of standards for the representation and interchange of data regarding Synthetic Environment Data Representation and Interchange Specification (SEDRIS). SISO is a membership organization that currently consists of 1131 members from 25 countries. The pre-history of SISO starts with SIMNET, a DARPA program from 1983 through 1991 that demonstrated the feasibility of networking substantial numbers of (relatively) low-cost simulators on a "virtual battlefield." Based on the success of this program, the US Army initiated a large-scale program called Combined Arms Tactical Training. In order to ensure that multiple teams of contractors would be able to bid on various components of this program, the Army Program Manager for Training Devices (PM TRADE), soon to be renamed as the Army Simulation Training and Instrumentation Command (STRICOM), in conjunction with DARPA and the newly established Defense Modeling and Simulation Office (DMSO), initiated a series of workshops at which user agencies and interested contractors could work together to develop standards based on the SIMNET protocols. The "First Conference on Standards for the Interoperability of Defense Simulations" was held on 22-23 August 1989 in Orlando, Florida.

Analysis. The field of operations research arose to address military applications, and there is still a major emphasis on using M&S to study the extremely complex problems of planning, organization, logistics, doctrine development, assessment of proposed new systems, etc.

Research and development. At every stage in the development of a new vehicle, weapon system, command and control system, etc., M&S is used for trade-off studies, design decisions, performance prediction, logistic support requirements, among many other uses.

Test and evaluation. As new systems are developed, they are tested first in M&S before they are taken onto physical test ranges, which are very expensive to operate. Interfaces with other systems are studied using M&S, and often other systems with which the new system must interact are represented in testing by simulations.

Training. Doctrines for how to use new systems are usually developed and tested via M&S. Then training simulations are developed for those who need to learn how to operate, support, maintain, or otherwise interact with these systems.

The "expensive" part of the problem arises not only because of the complexity of the simulations themselves, but also because of the many different types of simulations that need to be developed during the life cycle of a system. By and large, models and simulations of a new system are developed "from scratch" by each agency and contractor at each stage of system development, implementation, and use. Historically, there has been very little re-use of simulations across systems or across phases of development, so taxpayers have often paid for the creation of multiple simulations during each major system development program.

A related issue is the complexity of these simulations. In addition to making the simulations expensive, their complexity ensures that very few people have any deep understanding of the behavior of the simulations or the assumptions that go into developing them. In some cases, this lack of understanding, and the tremendous time and cost involved in developing a new simulation, have resulted in simulations being used for purposes beyond their scope of applicability. Sometimes this occurs as the result of a conscious decision to use an existing simulation rather than developing a new one; in other cases, it occurs as a result of lack of understanding of the limitations of a simulation. Since the late 1980's there have been serious efforts to address the related problems of expense and complexity by encouraging the development of simulations that are more modular and reconfigurable so that they can be reused for multiple purposes and multiple programs. SISO (and its predecessor organization) have played a major role in these efforts.

Consult http://www.sisostds.org/index.ph

Chronolgy of Modeling and Simulation Research and Tools

1952. The Society for Computer Simulation (SCS) was founded by John McLeod. Society activities, like conferences, publications, committees and working groups have been of great importance for the development of M&S methodology and software during the last five decades. SCS is a non-profit international association of men and women who are leaders in their professions: people who are responsible for creating new developments and applications in the rapidly expanding field of computer simulation. The SCS has American and European chapters and covers with its activities nearly all countries of the world. The McLeod Institute for Simulation Sciences is a part of the SCS, dedicated to research and academic issues. Each year the SCS organizes several simulation conferences in different countries. The most known publications of SCS are the journal Simulation and the Transactions of the Society for Computer Simulation (consult http://www.scs.org)

The McLeod Institute of Simulation Sciences (MISS) is a part of the Society for Computer Simulation International (SCS). The McLeod Institute was founded for the following reasons:

* To encourage and coordinate research and application in computer simulation
* To enhance opportunities for undergraduate and graduate teaching, research and training
* To stimulate the development, use, and evaluation of new instructional techniques and materials that make use of simulation.

The establishment of a center of the McLeod Institute of Simulation Sciences within a university or research center setting provides a mechanism through which faculty, students, and associates from various disciplines can bring their talents to bear in the general area of computer simulation or can apply simulation to new areas.

The Institute is named after Mr. John McLeod, P.E., the founder of the Society for Computer Simulation International and the founder and first editor of SIMULATION.

1961. Jay Forrester publishes his book "Industrial Dynamics." Then, the DYNAMO language appears (see previous sections).

1961. GPSS is developed (see previous sections).

1964. The CACI Company, founded in 1962, releases SIMSCRIPT. SIMSCRIPT II.5 is a powerful, free-form, English-like simulation language designed to greatly simplify writing programs for simulation modeling. SIMSCRIPT II.5 has been fully supported for over 40 years. The most important SIMSCRIPT features are:

DESIGN: A powerful world view, consisting of Entities and Processes, provides a natural conceptual framework with which to relate real objects to the model.

PROGRAMMING: SIMSCRIPT II.5 is a modern, free-form language with structured programming constructs and all the built-in facilities needed for model development. Model components can be programmed so they clearly reflect the organization and logic of the modeled system.

The amount of program needed to model a system is typically 75% less than in its FORTRAN or C counterpart.

DEBUGGER: A well designed package of program debug facilities is provided. The required tools are available to detect errors in a complex computer program without resorting an error. Simulation status information is provided, and control is optionally transferred to a user program for additional analysis and output.

EVOLUTION: This structure allows the model to evolve easily and naturally from simple to detailed formulation as data become available. Many modifications, such as the choice of set disciplines and statistics, are simply specified in the Preamble.

Contact: CACI Products Company, 3333 N Torrey Pines Ct, La Jolla, CA 92037, USA.

1967. Simula67 language is developed in the Norwegian Computer Center.

1967. Continuous System Simulation Language Committee of the Society for Computer Simulation (SCS) elaborates the standard in continuous simulation, named CSSL. This resulted in a whole family of languages, providing simulation software designed to assist engineers and scientists to mathematically model dynamic systems and to interactively conduct experiments on these models. CSSL-IV is a version of CSSL that includes a complete simulation environment, which facilitates rapid model definition, accurate experimentation, and graphic display of data.

CSSL IV provides advanced tools for nonlinear optimization, stiff equations integration, frequency response, spectral analysis and linear algebra. It also supports bond-graph front end.

An important product fully compatible with CSSL is the ACSL (Advanced Continuous Simulation Language), released by Mitchell and Gauthier Associates, Inc., 200 Baker Ave., Concord, MA 01742-2100, USA.

1975. SPICE package for electrical circuit analysis is developed at the University of California in Berkeley (see previous sections).

1979. A. Alan B. Pritsker develops SLAM, a general-purpose computer simulation language. SLAM relies heavily on GASP and Q-GERT, combining them to provide a single integrated framework.

Developed by Pritsker and Associates, SLAM II is the most known version of SLAM.

SLAM is an advanced FORTRAN-based language that allows simulation models to be built, using three different worldviews. It provides network symbols for building graphical models that are easily translated into input statements for direct computer processing. It contains subprograms that support both discrete event and continuous model development, and specifies the organizational structure for building such models. By combining networks, discrete event, and continuous modeling capabilities, SLAM allows the systems analyst to develop models from a process-interaction, next-event, or activity-scanning perspective. The interfaces between the modeling approaches are explicitly defined to allow new conceptual views of systems to be explored.

Consult: Pritsker (1984).

1983. The first release of the ANSYS software, by ANSYS Inc. ANSYS is a finite-element analysis package for distributed parameter systems, used widely in industry to simulate the response of a physical system to structural loading, and thermal and electromagnetic effects. ANSYS uses the finite-element method to solve the underlying governing equations and the associated problem-specific boundary conditions. The following list shows the date, product name, release and physics capability for the components of the ANSYS software.

1983, ANSYS/EMAG3D, 4.4, Low Frequency, statics

1997, ANSYS/EMAG3D, 5.4, Low Frequency, statics & High Frequency

2000 Q4, ANSYS/EMAG3D, 5.7, Low Frequency, statics & High Frequency, ANSYS/Multiphysics, High & Low Frequency

2001 Q4, ANSYS/EMAG3D, 6.0, Low Frequency, statics, ANSYS/Multiphysics, High & Low Frequency

2002 Q1, AI*EMAX , 6.0, High Frequency

2002 Q4, ANSYS EMAG, 7.0, Low Frequency, statics, ANSYS EMAX, High Frequency, ANSYS Multiphysics, High & Low Frequency

2003 Q2, ANSYS Emag, 7.1, Low Frequency, statics, ANSYS Emax, High Frequency & coupled thermal, ANSYS Multiphysics, High & Low Frequency

2003 Q4, ANSYS Emag, 8.0, Low Frequency, statics, ANSYS Emax, High Frequency & coupled thermal, ANSYS Multiphysics, High & Low Frequency

1984. The Math Works, Inc., releases MATLAB. It is a high-performance, interactive numeric computation and visualization environment that combines hundreds of advanced math and graphics functions with a high-level language. The open system architecture enables users to view the pre-packaged functions, customize these as needed, or add new functions. MATLAB toolboxes extend the power of the package by providing leading-edge algorithms and functions developed for signal processing, control system design, neural networks, optimization, and other applications. One of the most imporatnt parts of MATLAB is Simulink. This is a software package for continuous simulation of dynamic systems represented by block diagrams. Simulink is a part of the Matlab software family.

The Simulink model is created by dragging block icons into the screen. No written code is needed. More than 200 built-in block types are provided. The user can also design his/her own blocks with custom icons. Principal applications: control systems, signal processing.

Contact: The Math Works, Inc., 24 Prime Park Way, Natick, MA 01760, USA.

Mid-1980s. Mechanical Dynamics, Inc. develops ADAMS (Automatic Dynamic Analysis of Mechanical Systems).

ADAMS is a simulation package that enables engineers to parametrically model 3D mechanical systems and study alternative designs as "virtual prototypes." ADAMS simulations are used to evaluate system performance, range of motion, collision detection, packaging, peak loads, end FEA(Finite Element Analysis) input loads. Two-way interfaces with CAD, FEA, and control design packages are supported.

Contact: Mechanical Dynamics, Inc., 2301 Commonwealth Blvd., Ann Arbor, MI 48105, USA. In 2002, Mechanical Dynamics was acquired by MNS Software Company.

1986. CACI Company releases. Modsim II. This software provides libraries of objects that can be reused while creating new models. There is a graphical model editor that allows to graphically put the object icons and add parameters through dialog boxes

1988. The first release of the package Mathematica, by the Wolfram Research led by Stephen Wolfram. This is a fully integrated environment for technical computing. The concept of Mathematica was to create once and for all a single system that could handle all the various aspects of technical computing in a coherent and unified way. A new kind of symbolic computer language that could for the first time manipulate the very wide range of objects involved in technical computing, using only a fairly small number of basic primitives. Though this is not exactly a simulation package, the importance of the program for simulation applications cannot be overlooked. Mathematica's impact was felt mainly in the physical sciences, engineering, and mathematics.

Mid-1990s. SWARM package.

The basic objects in the Swarm system are agents, the simulated components. A schedule of discrete events on these objects defines a process occurring over time. In Swarm, individual actions take place at some specific time; time advances only by events scheduled at successive times. A schedule is a data structure that combines actions in the specific order in which they should execute. For example, the coyote/rabbit simulation could have three actions: "rabbits eat carrots," "rabbits hide from coyotes," and "coyotes eat rabbits." Each action is one discrete event: the schedule combines the three in a specific order, e.g. "each day, have the rabbits eat carrots, then they hide from the coyotes, then the coyotes try to eat the rabbits." The passage of time is modeled by the execution of the events in some sequence.

Consult: Minar, Burkhart, Langton and Askenazy (1996), and the page http://www.santafe.edu/projects/swarm/overview/overview.html.

1996. MODSIM III is released by the CACI Company. It is an environment for building advanced models. It generates readable C++ code, so the user can access libraries written in C++. The system under study is described as a collection of interacting objects. Each object module describes the object behaviors, called methods. Inheritance allows new objects to be defined as a special case of one or more general classes. The MODSIM concepts are similar to those of SIMULA, PASION and other object-oriented programming languages. The advantage of MODSIM is that it generates C code (Simula is based on Algol and PASION generates Pascal code).

1996. Integrated Systems company releases MATRIXx, a package for design automation and simulation. Oriented to automotive, aerospace, process control, servo design and other. Includes Xmath, an object-oriented analysis and visualization tool with a user-programmable GUI. Contact: Integrated Systems, 3260 Jay Street, Santa Clara, CA 95054, USA.

A remark on model existence

The existence of objects under consideration is one of the most important in scientific research. In fact, it seems that the only field where it is correctly stated and treated is mathematics. We should remember that looking for something that does not exist is one of the fundamental and fatal errors in any scientific research.

In this book, we will treat any invalid model as non-existent. The model validity is considered here as defined by Zeigler see section "Model validation." That definition of "absolute validity" may appear to be very theoretical and difficult to apply in practice. Note, however, that while it may be difficult to prove that a model is absolutely valid, the Zeigler definition can be applied in practice to prove that the consideren model is NOT valid (i.e. non-existent).

The validity of any model being designed for computer simulation, must be considered in the context of the corresponding experimental frame. In the section "Model validation" you can find an example of a model (two capacitors) that is valid in one experimental frame, and invalid in another. Here, we focus at some models that are commonly used, but which existence con be questioned. These are some models of soft systems, like population growth, Lotka-Voler5ra model and the models of epidemic spread. What we consider, is the existence of the ordinary differential equation (ODE) model for some of such systems.

To show how questionable is the existence of an ODE model, let us focus of the very beginning of the process of model building. For the ODE model, this stage is where the derivatives of state variables are defined. In many cases, it is assumed that the value of a derivative under consideration can be defined as a function of model state variables and external excitations. While such assumption is taken as an axiom, in fact, it may be false.

As an example, consider the Lotka-Volterra (L-V) model of a prey-predator system. Consider the changes of populations of two species: x – the predator (for example wolfs) and y – the prey (for example rabbits). To construct the L-V model the values of the derivatives of x and y are defined, as functions these two state variables.

The simplest L-V- model, without external input variables, is as follows:

$$\begin{cases} \dfrac{dx}{dt} = ax - bxy \\ \dfrac{dy}{dt} = cxy - dy, \end{cases} \qquad (1)$$

In the right-hand side of the first equation, the first term tells that the growth of the prey population is proportional to the population itself. The second term results from the assumption that the probability of contact prey-predator is proportional to the product xy. So, this term decreases the prey population. The second equation describes the changes in the predator population. This population may grow, when there is food (first term) and decreases according to the natural birth-and-death process (second term). Let us observe that the above assumptions, frequently taken as obvious, may be questioned. The simulation results of model (1) are described in section "Prey-predator model."

Other examples of an ODE model used in soft system modeling are the SIR, SIRS and similar models. The basic SIRS ODE model is as follows. (prime mark stands for time-differentiation). Here, S is the number of susceptible individuals, I is the number of infected and R is the number of recovered, see section "Epidemic spread."

$$\begin{cases} S' = \dfrac{-\beta SI}{N} + \xi R \\ I' = \dfrac{\beta SI}{N} - \gamma I \\ R' = \gamma I - \xi R \end{cases} \qquad (2)$$

In the above, β, ξ and γ are constants. The term ξR represents the number of recovered individuals that return to the S group. The state vector of this model is $X = (S, I, R)$. In the section "Epidemic spread" you can find examples of computer simulations of this model.

The above models, and their more sophisticated versions are widely used in modeling of ecological and epidemic dynamics research. There are many publications, where such models are considered valid because they fit to some real system data. Note, however, that the terms "widely used" and "widely known that…" are not scientific arguments. Until the end of the 19th century, it was well known that malaria disease was caused by "bad air." It was known as the Roman fever named after *mal'aria* ("bad air"), Several centuries ago, it was well known that the Sun moves over the (plain) Earth. As for the simulation models, the fact that the simulation results fit to some real data, does not mean that the model is valid. Our point is, that for the soft systems like prey-predator or epidemic spray, the ODE models do not exist at all. Let us see why these models are invalid, in the sense of "absolute" or "strict" validity defined by Zeigler.

First of all, models (1) and (2) do not reflect the spatial distribution of individuals. This, however, is frequently overcome by introducing some spatial-related components, or by looking for the governing partial differential equations.

Another, and the most important cause of ODE model nonexistence, is the huge collective memory that is present in any social dynamic system. This is a form of memory that is shared by a group and of central importance to the social identity of the group's members. This memory may store the information about the past behavioral patterns and about events, like diseases or predator attacks that affected the group. It can influence on the present and future behavior of the social group reflected, for example, in the collective evasive actions. The collective memory is a part of the system state. However, it can hardly be represented by a finite or even by a reasonably big number of the state variables.

While the problem of the spatial distribution of individuals can be overcome, there remain the following facts that make the ODE models like L-V and SIRS invalid.

1. In the above ODE models of soft systems, the model state is represented by two or three variables (L-V and SIRS). This way, the influence of the collective memory is ignored. Consequently, the right-hand sides of the equations (1) and (2) are undefined, and no corresponding ODE model exists.
2. Recall the definition of model validity, illustrated in figure 1 A. Here, X is the state of the real system, X_S is the state of the model, S is the operation of modeling (passing from the real system to the model), Y is the model output (observed variable), and t is the time. Function f represents the state transition. The model is considered valid, if the diagram of figure 1A commutes. In other words, passing from X(t) to $Y_S(t)$ we must obtain the same result, independently on the way we go. The same diagram, including the influence of the collective memory is shown in figure 1B. It can be seen, that, in this case, the diagram cannot commute, and the model is invalid or non-existing.

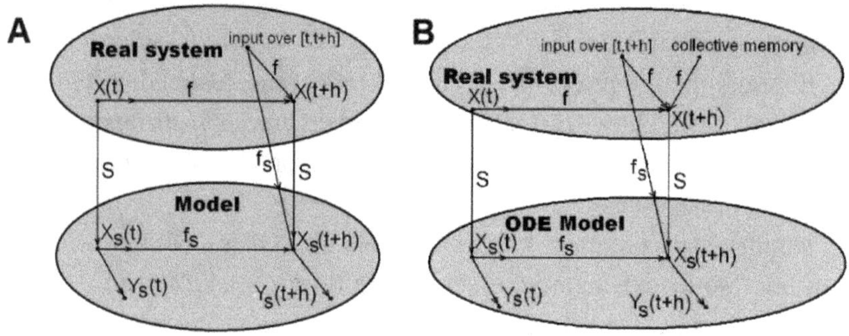

Figure 1.

Chapter 2

Continuous System Modeling & Simulation

General Remarks

Continuous simulation is the name given to the use of a computer to solve models with continuously changing states. Such models are generally composed of a number of differential equations. In the case of digital computer, these equations are solved numerically (P.Bratley, B.L. Fox and L.E.Schrage, *A guide to simulation,* Springer-Verlag, 1987).

In this part of the text, we discuss the principal mathematical tools: ordinary and partial differential equations and differential inclusions. More information on mathematical modeling is included in the section "Mathematical Tools."

Most of the continuous simulation models are based on ODE (ordinary differential equations). Recall that the ODEs work only if the real system can be simplified to a concentrated parameter one. In other words, if we model, for example, an electric circuit, all capacitances must be concentrated in ideal capacitor; all resistances must not have internal capacitance or inductance, etc. If there is at least one element like a "large line" where the signal propagates with finite velocity, the ODEs cannot be used. Other limitation for ODE model applicability is that the modeled system cannot have other memory than its state vector. This is the reason that the ODEs may fail while applied to complex tasks, like biomedical or ecological system simulation.

The widely known field of *System Dynamics* is nearly completely devoted to ODE modeling. Note that this approach has some risks. Indiscriminate use of ODE models to everything can lead to invalid models and wrong simulation results. First, few simulationists take care of the problem of the **existence** of the ODE model for a particular task.

Second, even if we find a corresponding differential equation, we must be sure that it has a solution (this is not always the case!). If the solution does not exist, the numerical method we apply can work, but the results may be wrong. Consult Raczynski S., *When System Dynamics ODE models fail,* SIMULATION, vol. 67, no.5, 1996.

Other kind of continuous dynamic systems are those of *distributed parameters.* The most typical examples are the temperature distribution problem, diffusion process, the string movement or fluid dynamics. Such models are described in terms of partial differential equations. Simulation of the distributed parameter systems is much more difficult that of the ODE models. There are many numerical methods that solve the PDEs, but all of them are rather time-consuming. Other approach is to divide the space where the process takes place into small *finite elements* and then describe the behavior of each element. This is implemented in many widely used methods of *finite element* that proved to be more effective than the numerical methods for the PEs

Analog Models and Simulation

A typical example of physical analog simulation is a wind-tunnel test on a scaled-down airplane physical model. Other way to do analog simulation is to look for an analogy between one physical model and another, for example a mechanical or electrical circuit. A simple electronic circuit with one operational amplifier, one resistance and one capacitor can realize the operation of mathematical integration. As a consequence, it is possible to solve differential equations using combinations of such circuits. The advanced devices with many such circuits and variable interconnections between them are called *analog computers*. It should be noted that the analog computers were (and still are) the unique devices that really solve differential equations. In digital computer nothing is continuous, and every numerical method for differential equations includes time-discretization and solves the equations with finite accuracy.

In early 40s and 50s analog computers were commonly used to simulate continuous dynamic systems, mainly automatic control, mechanical systems and others. During the ultimate decades analog computers have been losing importance because the differential equations they solve can be solved on digital computers with sufficient accuracy.

The operational amplifier is a device that amplifies electric signal in a wide frequency range, including frequency zero (direct current component). The amplifier has two input terminals> negative (inverting) and positive. It amplifies the difference of voltages at these two inputs. The gain of the amplifier negative and is very big, it reaches several thousand times, in the idealized amplifier it is supposed to be infinite. Below figure shows a typical applications: an inverting and integrator circuits. In the following examples the negative input is used.

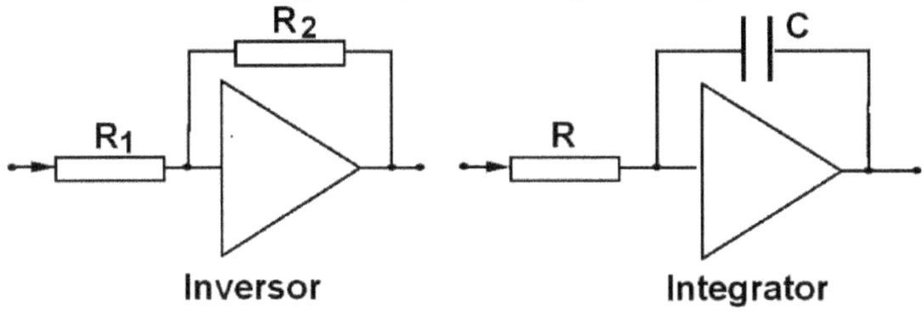

Inverting and integrating circuits.
The gain of the inversor is equal to -R_2/R_1.

Example

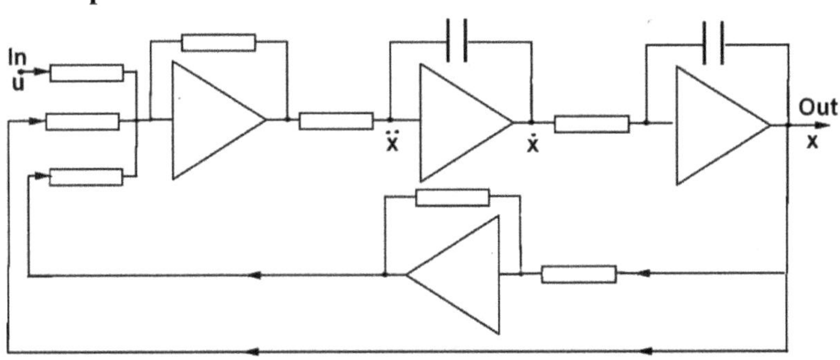

The above figure shows an analog circuit that satisfies the equation

$d^2x/dt^2 = -u - x - adx/dt$

where u(t) is an external input and x(t) is the model response. All amplifier inputs are supposed to have negative infinite gain. The rectangles represent resistances.

Ordinary Differential Equations

Let t be the independent variable, x be the dependent variable, and g be a scalar function of $n+1$variables. An ordinary differential equation of order n may have the following general form

$$g(x, x^{(1)}, x^{(2)}, \ldots, x^{(n)}, t) = 0 \text{ where } x^{(k)} = \frac{d^k x}{dt^k}, \quad x^{(0)} = x \tag{1}$$

Suppose that eq.(1) can be resolved with respect to $x^{(n)}$:

$$x^{(n)} = f(x, x^{(1)}, x^{(2)}, \ldots, x^{(n-1)}, t) \tag{2}$$

Now, define a vector $x=(x_0,x_1,, \ldots, x_{n-1})$ as follows.

$x_1=x,\ x_2=dx/dt,\ x_3=dx^2/dt^2, \ldots,\ x_n=d^{n-1}/dt^{n-1}$

With this notation, we obtain:

$$\begin{cases} dx_1/dt = x_2 \\ dx_2/dt = x_3 \\ dx_3/dt = x_4 \\ \ldots\ldots\ldots\ldots \\ dx_n/dt = f(x, x_1, x_2, \ldots\ldots, x_{n-1}) \end{cases} \tag{3}$$

Eq.(3) is the canonical form derived from eq(1). It is a set of n ordinary differential equations of the first order

More general form of this kind of equation is as follows.

$$\begin{cases} dx_1/dt = f_1(x, t) \\ dx_2/dt = f_2(x, t) \\ \ldots\ldots\ldots\ldots\ldots\ldots \\ dx_n/dt = fn(x, t) \end{cases}$$
$$x = (x_1, x_2, \ldots, x_n) \tag{4}$$

Or, in more compact form

$$\frac{dx}{dt} = f(x, t),$$
$$x = (x_1, x_2, \ldots, x_n), \quad f = (f_1, f_2, \ldots, f_n) \tag{5}$$

Vector x in (4) and (5) is also called the *state vector*, and the corresponding model is called *state-variable model.*

Example.

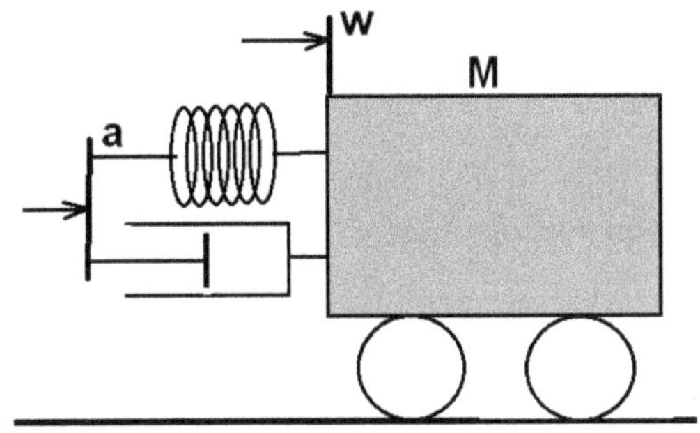

A mechanical system

Consider a mechanical system that includes a moving mass M, spring and damper, as above.

Here, *a* is the forced external displacement, and *w* is the mass position. The force produced at the spring is proportional to the spring length *w-a*, and the force of the dumper is determined by the speed of change of its length.

The governing equation is as follows.

$$K_1(a-w)+K_2(da/dt-dw/dt)-Md^2w/dt^2=0$$

Where K_1 is the spring constant, and K_2 is the dumper constant. The displacements are relative to the initial state with no forces and no movement.

Denoting $x_1=w$ and $x_2=d^2w/dt^2$ we obtain

$$\frac{dx_1}{dt}=x_2$$

$$\frac{dx_2}{dt}=(K_1(a-x_1)+K_2(da/dt-x_2))/M \tag{6}$$

The above equations describe the movement of the mass. The *state vector* of the system is $x=(x_1,x_2)$.

Differential Inclusions and Reachable Sets

Consider a mapping $F : Rn \times I \rightarrow P(Rn)$, where $P(X)$ denotes the power set, i.e., set of all subsets of the space X, I is an interval, $I \subset R$. A selection (or selector) of F over I is a function $z(t)$, such that $z(t) \in F(x, t) \forall t \in I$. Note that F is a *set-valued function.*

Differential Inclusion (DI) is defined by the following statement:

$$\frac{dx}{dt} \in F(x,t), \;\; x(0) \in X_0, \qquad (7)$$

Compare this with eq.(5). Instead of a vectorial function *f,* in the differential inclusion appears a set-valued function *F*. If the set *F* reduces to one point for all *t*, then the differential inclusion reduces to a differential equation. The present text is not on mathematics. So, we will not discuss more theoretical detail. For more information consult Raczynski S., "Reachable Sets of Dynamic Systems," Academic Press, 2023, ISBN-10 0443133840.

Let $I=[t_0,t_1]$ be a nonempty interval of the *t* axis. A function *z(t)* such that $z(t) \in F(x,t)$ for almost all $t \in I$ is called a *selector* of *F*. A function *x(t)* that satisfies inclusion (7) over *I,* with given initial condition is a *trajectory* of the inclusion (7). The *reachable or attainable set* of the inclusion (7) is the union of the graphs of all trajectories over I, with given initial condition or initial set.

Following figure shows an example of a 3D image of the reachable set obtained from the equations like those of the mass-spring-dumper (6). An uncertainty of parameters K_1 and K_2 were added, so that the right-hand side of (6) becomes a 2D set for each *x* and *t.*

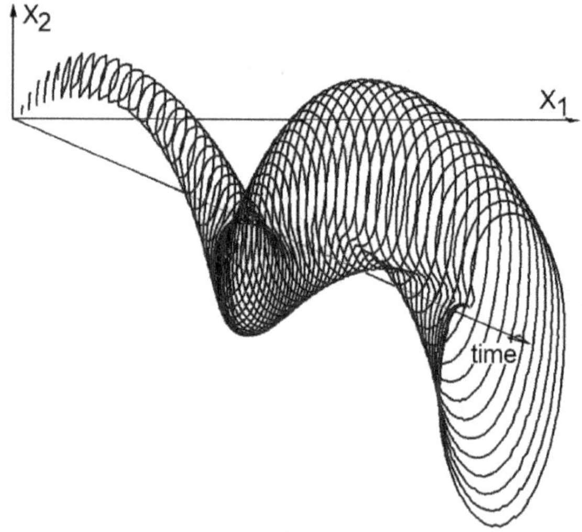

Example:
The reachable set of a second order dynamic system with uncertainty.

Differential Inclusion Solver

By solving the DI we mean finding its reachable set.

Somebody could expect that a solution algorithm for a DI might be obtained as some extension of known algorithms for differential equations. It might appear that trajectories generated randomly inside the reachable set (primitive simple shooting) can be used to estimate the shape of the reachable set. Unfortunately, this is not true. In the DI solver we calculate trajectories that scan the boundary of the reachable set, and not its interior. The trajectories should be uniformly distributed over the RS boundary. This can be done by random shooting of some kind, over the RS boundary. Such shooting has nothing to do with a simple or primitive random shooting, when the trajectories are generated randomly inside the RS. The general ideal of the solver is as follows.

We assume that the set F of (7) can be parametrized by an auxiliary variable u. This way, we obtain an equivalent control system, where the control variable belongs to a set of restrictions C(t). From the control theory it is known that if a trajectory reaches a point at the boundary of the set, it must entirely belong to the boundary. Such trajectories are optimal, according to certain optimality criterion (mainly time-optimal). So, we use the methods of the optimal control theory to generate such trajectories, see Raczynski S., (2002) "Differential Inclusion Solver." Conference paper: International Conference on Grand Challenges for Modeling and Simulation, The Society for Modeling and Simulation, San Antonio TX. for more detail. To compare the results of the simple shooting and the DI algorithm, consider the following DI:

$$\begin{cases} \dfrac{dx}{dt} = F(x) \\ F = \{z : z = u - x_1 - 1.2\,|x_2|,\, u \in [-1, 1]\} \\ where \quad x = (x_1, x_2). \end{cases} \tag{8}$$

The following figure shows the contour of the reachable set for system (8). The "simple shooting" is the result of integrating 10000 trajectories, while the contour found by the solver contains only 500 trajectories. Simulation final time is equal to 50.

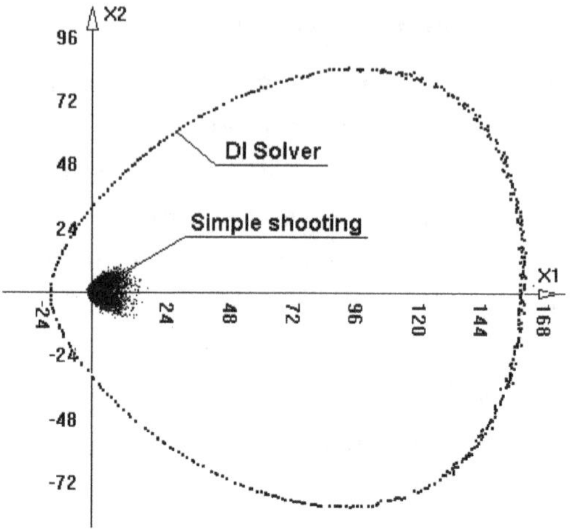

An example of the contour of the reachable set.

Functional Sensitivity and reachable sets

Unlike the classic sensitivity definition, we define the functional sensitivity in terms of the calculus of variations. It is pointed out that the non-local functional sensitivity is given in the form of the system reachable set. The solution to the functional sensitivity is shown, using the differential inclusion solver that calculates and displays the system reachable set.

Conventional sensitivity

First, recall the conventional sensitivity concepts (SA). There are many kinds of such analysis, as listed below.

Scatter plots represent a useful tool in the SA. Plots of the output variable against individual input variables are displayed. This gives us a graphical view of the model sensitivity. View Friendly and Denis (2005) for more detail.

Regression analysis is a powerful tool for sensitivity problems. It allows us to examine the relationship between two or more variables of interest. The method is used to model the relationship between a response variable and one or more external variables or perturbations. Consult, for example, Freedman (2005) or Cook (1092).

Sobol method and Screening are useful tools in the variance-based modeling. It decomposes the variance of the output of the model or system into fractions which can be attributed to the input or sets of inputs. Thus, we can see which variable is contributing significantly to the output uncertainty in high-dimensionality models. For more detail, see Morris (1991) and Sobol (1993).

Logarithmic gain is a normalized sensitivity defined by the percentage response of a dependent variable to an infinitesimal change in an independent variable. In dynamical systems, the logarithmic gain can vary with time, and this time-varying sensitivity is called dynamic logarithmic gain. This concept is used in dynamic sensitivity analysis, where the core model is a dynamic system, described by ordinary differential equations. Consult Sriyudthsak et al. (2015).

The **System Dynamics** software (Forrester (1961)) offers tools for dynamic sensitivity analysis. Programs like Vensim or PowesSim include procedures that generate multiple model trajectories when the selected model parameters vary from one trajectory to another. However, in these packages, the parameters are constants along the trajectory.

Our approach is different. As explained in the following sections, we treat both the perturbations and uncertain model parameters as functions of time. Instead of the classical sensitivity concept, we use the functional sensitivity, defined in the following sections. The main tool used here is the differential inclusion solver that calculates model reachable sets (see Raczynski (2002)).

Functional sensitivity

The classical, local sensitivity analysis (basic local version) uses the partial derivatives of the model output Y, with respect to components of an input vector (model parameters) $u = (u_1, u_2, ..., u_n)$, at a given point u_0:

$$\left|\frac{\partial Y}{\partial u_i}\right|_{u_0} . \qquad (1)$$

The derivative is taken at some fixed point in the space of the input (hence the "local" in the name of the analysis mode). The use of partial derivatives suggests that we consider small perturbations of the input vector, around the point of interest u_0. Consult Cacuci (2003). Consider a dynamic model described by an ordinary differential equation

$$\frac{dx}{dt} = f(x, u, t), \qquad (2)$$

where $x = (x_1, x_2, ..., x_n)$ is the state vector, $u = (u_1, u_2, ..., u_m)$ is the perturbation (parameters, control) vector, and t is the time. We have $x \in X$, $u \in U$, $f: X \times U \times R \rightarrow X$. Here, X is the state space, U is the control space, and R is the real number space. We restrict the considerations to the case $X = R^n, U = R^m$, $R = R^1$, R^k being the real Euclidean k-dimensional space. Let $t \in I = [0, T]$, and G be the space of all measurable functions u: $I \rightarrow R^m$.

Now, consider a variation δ u of u and a perturbed control u∗. The variation is a function of time, so that

$u'(t) = u(t) + \delta u(t) \; \forall t \in I$

(prime mark is not the time differentiation). The solution to (2) over I, with given initial condition $x = x_0$ and given function $u(*)$, will be called a trajectory of (2). Thus, any component x_k of the final value of $x(t)$ depends on the shape of the whole function $u(*)$. In other words, $x_k(t) = x_k(t)[u\_]$ is a functional (not a function) of $u\_ (*)$. Unlike a function, in our case, the functional is a mapping from the space G to R. Denote $\delta x_k = x_k [u + \delta u] - x_k [u] = x_k [u\_] - x_k [u]$.

We define the local functional sensitivity as follows:

$$S_k = \left| \frac{\delta x_k}{\delta u_0} \right| . \qquad (3)$$

Note the difference between the conventional local sensitivity (1) and the functional sensitivity (3). The notation δu denotes the variation of the function u, as defined in the calculus of variations (see Nearing (2010) and Elsgolc (2007)). A variational approach to sensitivity is also discussed in Arora (2012), Mordukhovich (2005), and Sriyudthsak (2015). The term (3) defines a local property of the trajectory $x_k(t)$. Here, we are interested rather in the response of the model to perturbations that are not necessarily small. We will not enter in the methodology of the variational calculus.

Our task is to define the functional sensitivity as the set of the graphs of all trajectories of (2), where $u = u_0 + \_u$. Here, $\_u(t)$ is a limited perturbation, not necessarily small. Considering the control system (2), this is equivalent to say that *u(t)* belongs to the set of restrictions *C(x, t)*, $u(t) \in C(x, t), \forall t \in I$. Here, *C(x, t)* is a subset of R^m. When *u* scans all possible values inside the set *C*, then the right-hand side of (4.4) defines a set-valued function. This way, (2) with disturbed control also defines the corresponding differential inclusion. The functional sensitivity defined this way is non-local. We do not use the term "global," because this is not a global property of the model. We just do not require the perturbation to be small. Models with uncertain parameters and control systems are closely related to differential inclusions. Consider a model defined as follows (Eq. 4):

$$\frac{dx}{dt} = f(t, x(t), u(t)), \quad x(t) \in R^n, \quad u(t) \in C(x, t), \quad t \in I = [t_0, T], \quad t_0 < T, \tag{4}$$

where R^n is the real n-dimensional Euclidean space, $x \in R^n$, $u \in R^m$, *t* is a real variable representing the time, and *C* represents the restrictions for variable *u*. Equation (3) may represent a control system with control variable *u*, as well as a model with uncertain variable parameters *u*. When *u* scans all possible values in *C*, then the right-hand side of (4.6) scans the values inside a set *F*. This defines the corresponding differential inclusion, as follows:

$$\frac{dx}{dt} \in F(t, x). \tag{5}$$

Here, $F(t, x) = \{z : z = f(t, x, u), u \in C(x, t)\}$. This way,we obtain a differential inclusion (5). More detailed assumptions and a comprehensive survey on differential inclusions can be found in Aubin and Cellina [1].

Example: A control system

Functional sensitivity can be an important tool in robust control system design. Such systems should not only be stable and perhaps optimal, but also must work satisfactory with adverse external disturbances. For more information on robust control consult, for example, Xu and Lam (2006) or Zhou and Doyle (1997). Figure 1 shows a closed-loop control system. The controller is of the proportional–derivative–integral action, and the process is of second order, oscillatory. The set point is denoted as *p*, *e* is the control error, *z* is a disturbance, *q* and *x* are the process input and output, respectively. The control error $e = p - x$. Two versions of the controller are used: the classic PID and the anti-windup version. At the controller output, there is an actuator that may saturate when its limit L is reached.

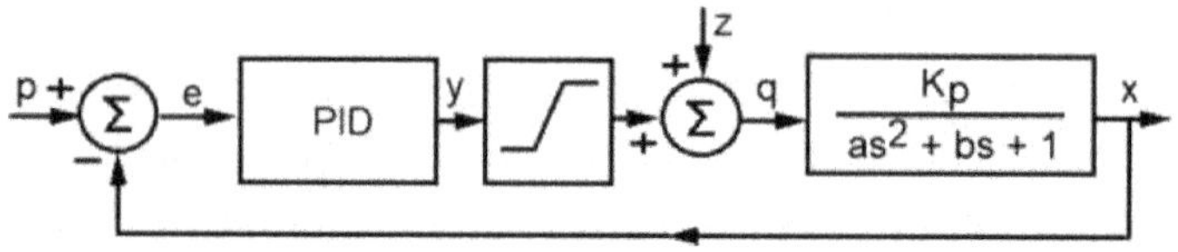

Figure 1. A closed-loop control system with PID controller

The classic PID is described by the following equation (in terms of the Laplace transform).

$$y(s) = K_R e(s)\left(1 + T_d s + \frac{1}{T_i s}\right), \tag{6}$$

where K_R is the controller gain, Ti is the integrator parameter (duplication time), and T_d is the derivative action parameter. To avoid differentiation of the set-point signal that may have discontinuities, we use the controller where the set point is not applied to the differentiator (a special case of the "set-point weighing").

$$y(t) = K_R\left(e(t) - T_d \frac{dx}{dt} x + \frac{1}{T_i}\int_0^t e(\tau)d\tau\right), \tag{7}$$

where the error $e = p - x$ is replaced by $-dx/dt$. The controlled process is described by the following equation:

$$a\frac{d^2x}{dt^2} + b\frac{dx}{dt} + x(t) = K_R q. \tag{8}$$

Further analysis of the system requires the canonical (vectorial) form of the model equations. To obtain this for equations, first let us denote

$$g(t) = \frac{1}{T_i}\int_0^t e(\tau)d\tau. \tag{9}$$

Now, we define the state vector (x_1, x_2, x_3), so that

$$x_1 = x,\ x_2 = dx/dt\ ,\ x_3 = g. \quad (10)$$

From (7), (8), and (10), we obtain

$$\begin{cases} \dfrac{dx_1}{dt} = x_2 \\ \dfrac{dx_2}{dt} = (K_p(y+z) - bx_2 - x_1)/a \\ \dfrac{dx_3}{dt} = \dfrac{v}{T_i}(p - x_1) \\ \dfrac{dx_4}{dt} = \dfrac{dg}{dt} = K_R(e - T_d x_2 + x_3). \end{cases} \quad (11)$$

The variable v is added to simulate the anti-windup PID controller. This PID version is implemented to avoid the windup effect, when the value of the integration action may become very large. This occurs when the control error is positive or negative during long time interval. In practical applications, due to the windup, the actuator limit may be reached and the control signal y becomes constant. There are several analog versions of the anti-windup controller (consult Astrom and Hagglund (1995)). However, in newer PID implementation, the anti-windup is done by software. It turns off the integration action when the saturation occurs. The variable v is defined as follows:

$$v(e, y, L) = \begin{cases} 0 \text{ if } |y| \geq L \\ 1 \text{ if } |y| < L \text{ or } (y \geq L \text{ and } e < 0) \text{ or } (y \leq -L \text{ and } e > 0). \end{cases} \quad (12)$$

where L is the saturation level. Variable v shuts down the integrator action when the saturation level is reached and turns it ON when the integrated value is equal or greater than L, and e is negative, or when the integrated value is equal or lower than $-L$ and e is positive.

As stated before, the functional sensitivity is given by the reachable set of the model.

Consider the model (11). The parameters are as follows:

$a = 2,\ b = 1$ (process parameters),

$p = 1$ (the set point),

$K_R = 2.5$ (controller gain),

$T_i = 2$ (duplication time),

T_d= 0.2 (derivative time),

L = 1.6 (actuator saturation level).

The above PID settings are not optimal. They were defined this way, to exaggerate some imperfections in the transient process. Anyway, a robust control system should work not only with optimal parameters.

Suppose that both the values of the disturbance z and the process gain K_R are uncertain and may fluctuate by ±20% around their original values. The system response reaches a steady state after about 30 time units. However, we are interested rather in system behavior during the transient process, so we will investigate the functional sensitivity at shorter time, t = 8.

Figure 2 shows the reachable set of the process response to unit step input, process only, open loop. In Fig. 3, we can see some, randomly selected (but not random), trajectories that scan the boundary of the reachable set for process only. Now, let the same parameter fluctuations be applied in the closed-loop control circuit. First, we simulate the system without actuator saturation. The closed-loop model is of order three. Thus, the reachable set boundary at a given final time instant is not just a contour, but a three-dimensional cloud of points. The points are located on a three-dimensional surface, like a surface of a balloon. Consequently, we cannot get a two-dimensional contour. We can only see projections of the reachable set boundary into a two-dimensional plane. The DI solver generates a lot of such projections. Let us show only an example, namely, the projections into the plane $x_1 - x_3$ and $time - x_1$.

Figure 4 shows the projection of the reachable set at t = 8 into the plane $x_1 - x_3$. Figure 5 depicts the “side view” of the same reachable set, projected into the $time - x1$ plane.

The functional sensitivity analysis can provide important information to be used in robust control design. It can be seen that the functional sensitivity sets are larger than those provided by the classic sensitivity analysis.

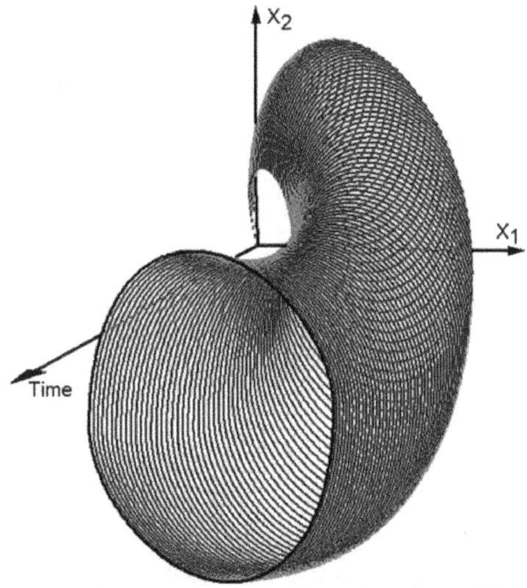

Figure 2. The 3D image of the functional sensitivity of the controlled process in open loop, (reachable set)

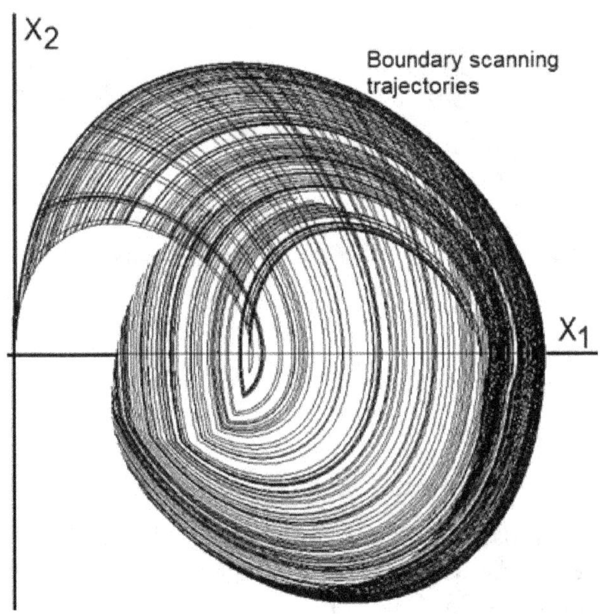

Figure 3. Some boundary-scanning trajectories, process in open loop

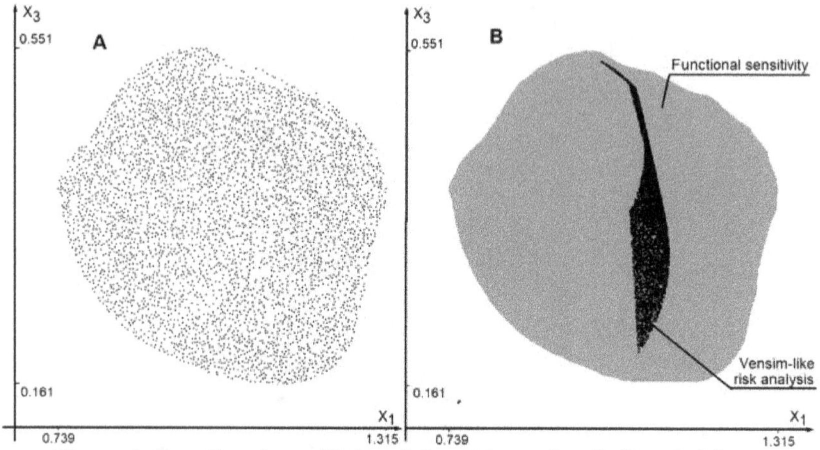

Figure 4. Functional sensitivity of closed-loop circuit. Reachable set at t = 8, anti-windup controller, saturation level 1.6

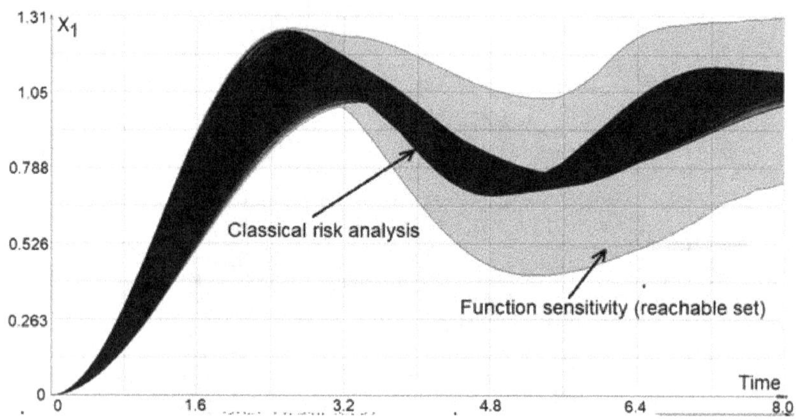

Figure 5. Projection of the reachable set into the *time* − x_1 plane. Anti-windup controller, saturation level equal to 1.6

References (Functional sensitivity)

Arora J.S., Cardoso JB (2012) Variational principle for shape design sensitivity. Aerosp Res Central 30(2):538–547, AIAA. https://doi.org/10.2514/3.10949

Astrom K.J., Hagglund T (1995) PID controllers. Instrument Society of America, ISBN: 1-55617-516-7

Cacuci D.G. (2003) Sensitivity and uncertainty analysis. Chapman&Hall/CRC, London. ISBN:
1-58488-115-1

Cook R.D., Weisberg S (1982) Criticism and influence analysis in regression. Sociol Methodol 13:313–461

Elsgolc L.D. (2007) Calculus of variations. ISBN: 978-0486457994

Forrester J.W. (1961) Industrial dynamics. Pegasus Communications, Waltham, MA

Freedman D.A. (2005) Statistical models: theory and practice. Cambridge University Press

FriendlyM, and Dennis D.(2005) The early origins and development of the scatterplot. JHist Behav Sci 41(2):103–130. https://doi.org/10.1002/jhbs.20078

Mordukhovich (2005) Sensitivity analysis for generalized variational and hemivariational inequalities. Adv Anal 305–314. https://doi.org/10.1142/9789812701732_0026

MorrisM.D. (1991) Factorial sampling plans for preliminary computational experiments. Technometrics 33:161–174. https://doi.org/10.2307/1269043

Nearing J. (2010) Mathematical tools for physics. Dover Publications

Raczynski S. (2002) Differential inclusion solver. In: Conference paper: conference paper: international conference on grand challenges for modeling and simulation, The Society for Modeling and Simulation Int., San Antonio TX

Sobol I. (1993) Sensitivity analysis for non-linear mathematical models.Math Modeling Comput Exp 1:407–414

Sriyudthsak K., Uno H, Gunawan R, Shiraishi F (2015) Using dynamic sensitivities to characterize metabolic reaction systems. Math Biosci 269:153–163

Takeuchi Y. (1996) Global dynamical properties of Lotka-Volterra systems. World Scientific

Xu S, Lam J. (2006) Robust control and filtering of singular systems. Springer. https://doi.org/10.1007/11375753

Zhou K. and Doyle J.C. (1997) Essentials of robust control. Prentice Hall, ISBN: 0-13-525833-2

Bond Graphs

Bond graph method, introduced by Paynter in 1961 (Paynter H.M., *Analysis and design of engineering systems,* MIT Press, Cambridge, Mass., 1961), is the widespread tool in modeling of physical systems. The fact that a bond connects two variables: the effort and the flow, makes this tool the most appropriate for physical systems modeling because the flow of power is the product of these two variables (e.g. voltage and current, force and velocity, liquid pressure and flow etc.). An excellent overview of bond graphs can be found in Francois Cellier, *Hierarchical non-linear bond graphs: a unified methodology for modeling complex physical systems,* SIMULATION, April 1992. Recall that a bond graph model is composed by the nodes or junctions and by the links named bonds. A bond is a directed link with a harpoon. The harpoon is placed on the left of the link (related to its direction). The two variables are indicated as follows. The effort is placed on the side of the harpoon and the flow is indicated on the other side.

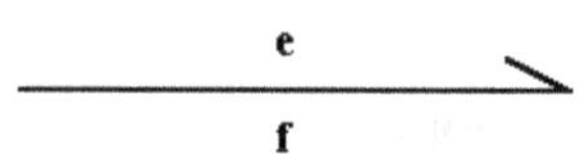

There are several types of nodes in bond graph models. At the node of type 0 the sum of flows is equal to zero, while the efforts of all connected bonds are equal to each other. At the node of type 1 the sum of efforts must be zero and the flows of all corresponding bonds are the same. Thus, we can represent graphically any system that obeys a number of balance equations.

The node equations for the node 0 and the node 1 are as follows.

f - g - h = 0 (node of type 0)

e - v - w = 0 (node of type 1)

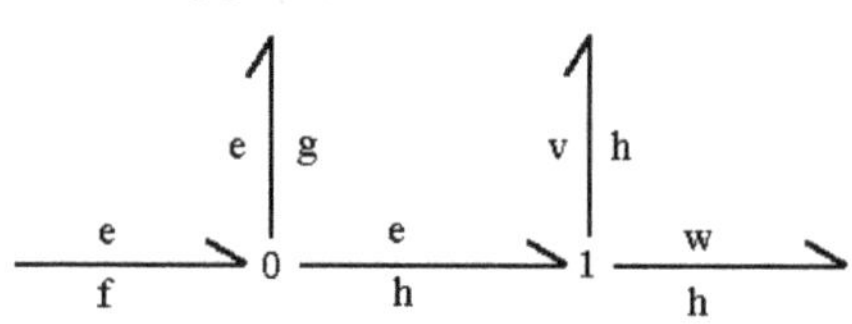

The sign of a term in the node equation depends on the direction of the corresponding bond, the outgoing bond having the negative sign of the corresponding variable. Other possible nodes accepted by BOND are as follows.

SE node - effort source, for example an external force, ideal voltage source, etc.

SF node - flow source, e.g. mandated velocity in a translational system, ideal current source.

R node - dissipative element, e.g. damper or electrical resistance

C node - capacitance, e.g. a spring or electrical capacitance L/I node - Inertia/inductance, for example a moving or rotating mass, electrical inductance.

The causality in bond graph diagrams is denoted by a stroke at one of the ends of the bond. This means that the flow variable is evaluated at the end with the stroke, and the effort variable at the other end.

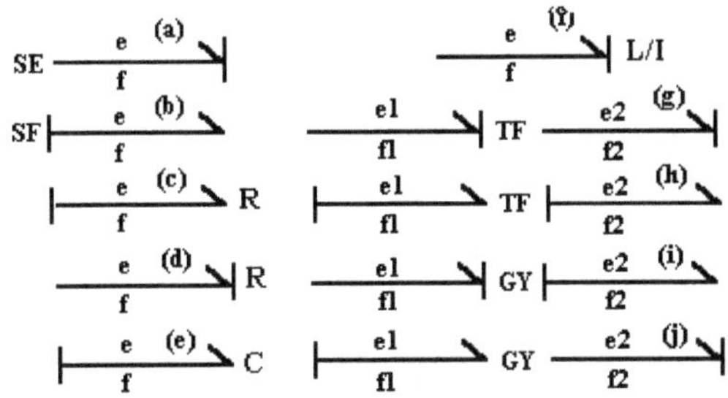

The above figure shows the possible combinations of bonds and nodes of type SE, SF, R, L/I and C accepted by the BOND program and the implied causalities. All free ends of the bonds can be connected to nodes of type 0 or 1.

The node-bond combinations of are:

(a) (SE node) Effort source. The effort e is defined at the node.

(b) (SF node) Flow source. The flow f is defined.

(c),(d) (R node) Dissipative bonds. The equations are

f = e/R and e = fR , respectively.

(e) (C node) Capacitance. It has the desired causality as shown. The equation is

de/dt = f/C , C being the capacitance

(f) (I/L node) Inertia or Inductance. The equation is

df/dt = e/L , L is a constant (mass, inductance etc.)

(g) (TF bond) Ideal transformer. The equations are

e1 = m e2 , f2 = m f1 , m is a constant

(h) (TF bond) Ideal transformer. The equations are

e2 = e1/m , f1 = f2/m , m is a constant

(i) (GY bond) Ideal "gyrator." The equation is

e1 = rf2, e2 = rf1, r is a constant

(j) (GY bond) Ideal "gyrator." The equation is

f2 = e1/r, f1 = e2/r, r is a constant

Note that R node-bond combination and the TF and GY bonds have two possible causalities, while the other bonds must have the causalities indicated in the previous figure. These causalities may be given by the user. However, any graph is scanned by BOND in order to check and, if necessary, to change or add the causalities. If the user causalities are wrong they are changed and the corresponding message appears. If BOND cannot find a solution (causality conflict), the analysis stops and the error message is issued.

The bond direction always can be inverted, which merely changes the sign of both variables. However, we will require that the bonds connected to the R, C and L/I nodes come into these nodes, and the bonds connected to SE and SF nodes go out of them.

EXAMPLE

Consider a simple mechanical system shown below

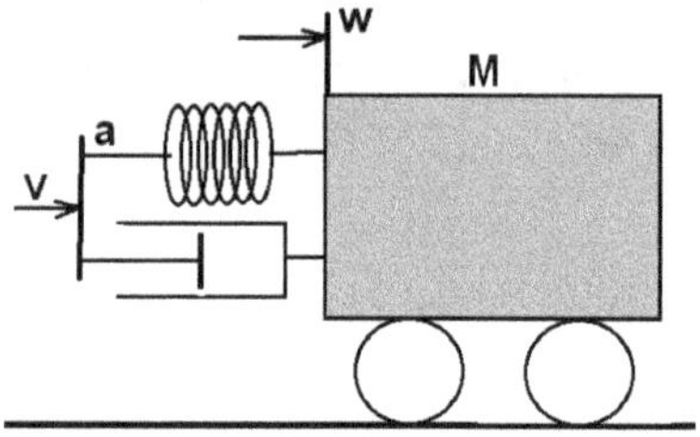

Here, v is the velocity of the point a, w is the car velocity and M is the mass of the car.

The corresponding bond graph is shown on the following figure where

$px = v - w$

g is the force of the damper

f is the applied force on the mass

hx is the force of the spring

Recall that in mechanical systems the efforts are forces and flows are velocities. (This is an example of the PSM++ BONDW model.

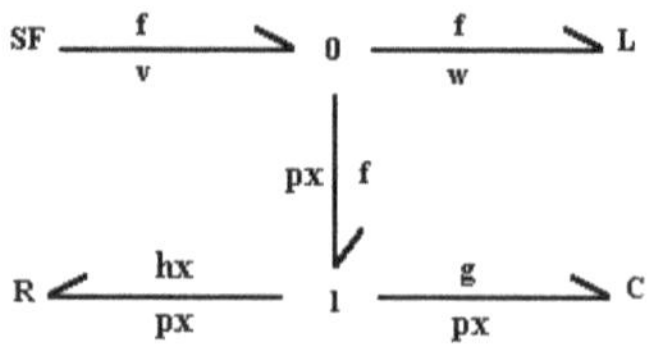

Signal Flow Diagrams

This a graphical representation of dynamic systems, mostly used in continuous system modeling. The graph is constructed using nodes (represented by points) and directed links between nodes, represented by arrows. The nodes represent signals (functions of time) and the links are corresponding transfer functions or more general operators that convert the input signal (the arrow starting point) into the output signal (the arrow head). A node with no arrows pointing to it is a *source node*. At least one source node should exist in a signal flow graph. The analytic tool that can be used to determine the transfer function for the whole graph is known as the Mason rule (consult Richard Dorf, *Modern Control Systems,* Addison-Wesley, 1992, sec. 2.7).

Signal-flow graphs are useful in modeling automatic control systems, instrumentation, and causal physical systems

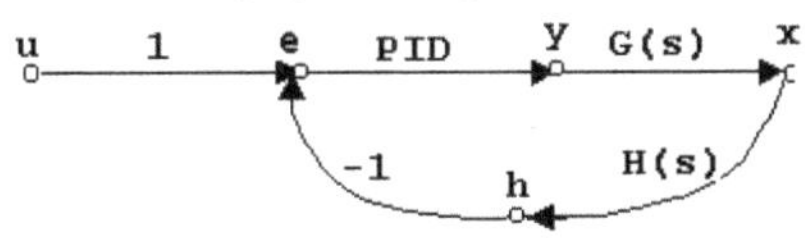

The above graph describes a model of a feedback control system. Node ***u*** is the set point, ***e*** is the control error, ***y*** is the controller output signal, ***x*** is the controlled variable, and ***h*** is the measurement of **x**. At the node **e** the control error is calculated, ***e* = *u* - *h*.** PID is the transfer function of a PID controller, *G(s)* represents the controlled process, and *H(s)* is the dynamics of the measurement instrument. The following figure shows a simple circuit with an operational amplifier (a follower) and the corresponding signal flow graph.

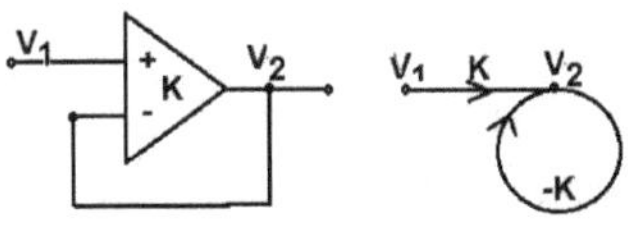

While used for computer simulation, the links can be linear as well as non-linear components, delays, sample-and-hold or even entire sub-models defined earlier.

There is simulation software that facilitates the use of signal flow graphs. The user defines the graph on the screen using the mouse, gives the model parameters and the software does the rest. Namely, the software generates the system differential equations, source program code, compiles and runs it. Consult *BLUESSS* .

Example: Car suspension

Consider a car that moves forward and faces the road irregular shape. Thus, the car suspension receives a (nearly) vertical excitation form the point where the tire touches the ground. From the point of view (reference) of the driver, the car velocity is equal to zero and the road moves backwards in the diver-related coordinates. In a simplified model, the dynamics is considered only in vertical direction, supposing that the suspension supports a "quarter car." In this model we have one wheel with the tire, spring and shock absorber. Such model provides an important information about the movements, though the three-dimensional movement is ignored. If we use the complete system model, with four or more wheels, we must treat the car as a rigid body. This complicates the model, but may provide information about the car real movement and its stability. Another difficulty is the way to display and interpret the results. The general properties and suspension types are described briefly in "The Suspension Bible," available from the Web. A simple simulation can provide an interesting view on the behavior of the suspension. The differential inclusion model may provide more information about possible extreme system behavior, important in the security issues.

Suppose that the car moves forward with a constant horizontal velocity V. Thus, taking the car position as the reference and considering all variables as differences between their actual values and the initial equilibrium state, we take into account the following variables.

y - the movement of the wheel

x - movement of the vehicle

F_1 - the force determined by the compliance of the tire

F_2 - the force of the suspension spring

F_a - the force produced by the damper

u - an external excitation, due to the shape of the road

All the above variables are functions of time and all represent vertical movements and forces. The following figure shows the corresponding mechanical scheme.

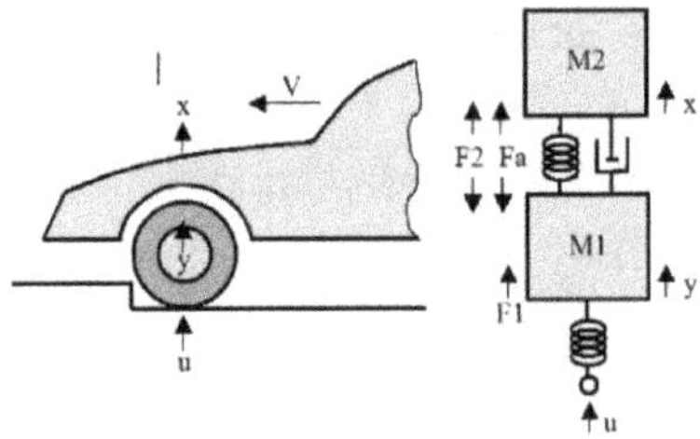

Car suspension scheme.

M_1 and M_2 are the mass of the wheel (together with the moving part of the suspension) and the mass of the car, respectively (M2 being 1/4 of the car total mass).

To derive the model equations, we must use the force balance for the two masses, including the dynamic forces. This provides the following equations.

$$F_1 - F_2 - F_a - M_1 d^2y/dt^2 = 0$$
$$F_2 + F_a - M_2 d^2x/dt^2 = 0 \qquad (1)$$

The force of the two springs and of the damper depend on the corresponding changes of the spring and damper length, so

$$F_1 = K_1(y-u), \quad F_2 = K_2(x-y)$$
$$F_a = K_a(dx/dt - dy/dt) \qquad (2)$$

Note that the damper force depends on the velocities and not positions. The above force are supposed to be linear with respect to the positions and velocities. Further on, we will discuss a more realistic version includes non-linear functions for the force. We convert the above equations to the canonical form of four equations of the first order, using the following notation.

$$x_1=x,\ x_2=dx/dt,\ x_3=y,\ x_4=dy/dt$$

After substituting the new variables into (2) and reordering the equations, we obtain the following.

$$dx_1/dt = x_2$$
$$dx_2/dt = [K_2(x_3-x_1)+K_a(x_4-x_2)]/M_2$$
$$dx_3/dt = x_4$$
$$dx_4/dt = [K_1(u(t)-x_3)-K_2(x_3-x_1)-K_a(x_4-x_2)]/M_1 \qquad (3)$$

The last set of equations can be used to simulate our system. Note that we obtain four equations, and that the state vector of the model is $\boldsymbol{x} = (x_1,$

$x_2, x_3, x_4)$. This is correct because the movement equation for each mass is of the second order.

The model (3) is a simple linear version of the suspension movement. We start with this model, to assess the appropriate value of the dumping coefficient K_a.

In the first simulation, the system parameters are as follows.

$M1$ = 25 Kg, $M2$ = 200 Kg, $K1$ = 100000 N/cm, $K2$ = 22000 N/cm. The external excitation $u(t)$ is a step function with amplitude 10cm, starting at t=0 (the car enters an obstacle or sidewalk 10 cm high). Note that we use the SI unit system, the mass in Kg, the velocity in m/sec and the force in newtons. The first simulation was run with Ka=200 N/(m/sec). The position of the car body and the wheel can be seen in figure following figure. The values are relative, with respect to the initial positions in the steady state equilibrium.

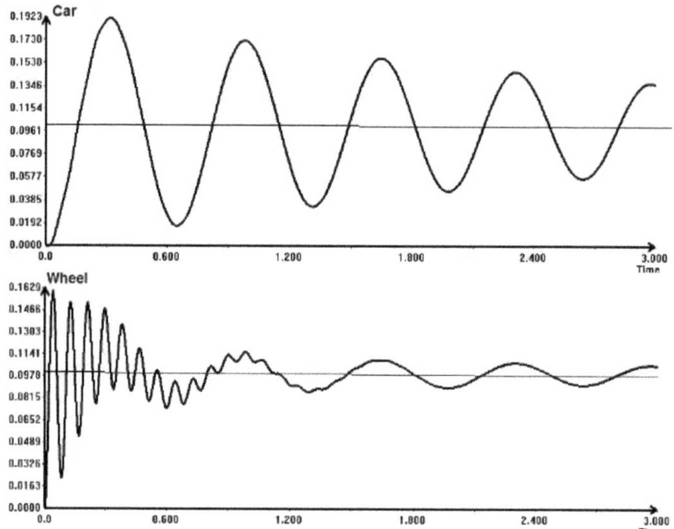

Car suspension simulation with the shock absorber coefficient equal to 200 N/(m/sec).

The results with Ka=200 N/(m/sec) are not satisfactory. It is supposed that the driver should not detect more than three oscillations after entering an obstacle. Such a permissible case is reached with Ka=1400, as shown below.

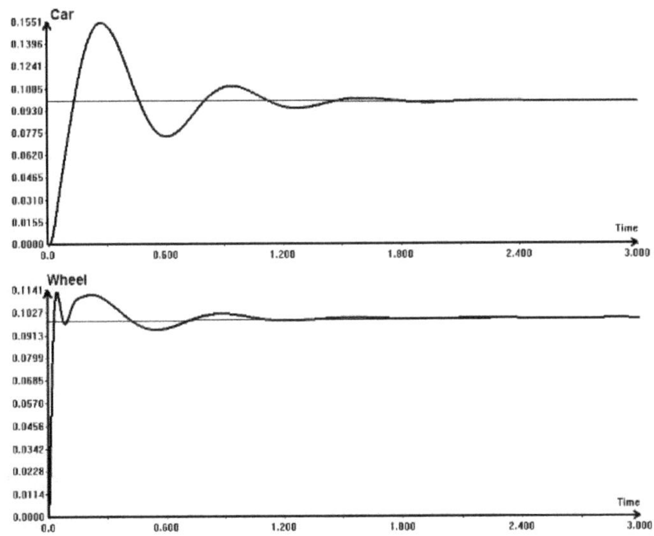

Simulation results with shock absorber coefficient equal to 1400 N/(m/sec). The function u(t) is constant, equal to 0.1m.

It can be seen that both the wheel and the car "jump" upwards by 10cm. The wheel position has oscillations with the dominant frequency higher than the car body. Anyway, both curves represent a superposition of two frequencies.

Prey-Predator model

Here, we discuss some properties of the ordinary differential equation (ODE) model of a soft, namely the prey-predator system. However, our point is that such model may be invalid, or non-existent. Consult the section "A remark on model existence" for more detail about this issue.

The classic model of the prey-predator system is described by Lotka-Volterra (L-V) equations. In the simplest case of two species, the prey population (for example rabbits) grows according to the birth-and-death process. The growth would be exponential, but there is a limitation: the predators (e.g. wolves) are eating rabbits. The population of wolves grows when they have food, but if there are few rabbits available, the wolves die. Denote the rabbit population size as x_1 and the wolves as x_2. The classic form of two-species Lotka-Volterra equations is as follows.

$$\frac{dx_1}{dt} = ax_1 - bx_1x_2$$
$$\frac{dx_2}{dt} = -cx_2 + dx_1x_2 \qquad (1)$$

In the first equation, the term bx_1x_2 means that the rate of rabbits caught by wolves is proportional both to the number of wolves and to the number of rabbits. A similar term appears in the second equation. The growth rate of wolves increases when they have more food. Coefficient a defines the rabbits natural growth rate, and c defines the wolves natural death rate. This is the *basic L-V model*. There are many other versions of the equations used in ecological models, with two or more species in the N-species food chains. Consult Takeuchi Y. (1996) Global Dynamical Properties of Lotka-Volterra Systems. World Scientific, Lotka A.J. (1910) Contribution to the Theory of Periodic Reaction. 14(3):271-274 and Cropp R.A., Norbury J. (2015) Population Interactions in Ecology: A Rule-Based Approach to Modeling Ecosystems in a Mass-Conserving Framework. SIAM REVIEW, Society for Industrial and Applied Mathematics, 57(3):437-465.

In the real system, the amount of prey and predator are integer numbers. In the continuous L-V equations, the variables are interpreted as averages. Nowak (2006), gives an outline of the mathematical principles of evolution of species. The book introduces readers to the powerful yet simple laws that govern the evolution of living systems, no matter how complicated they might seem. Another recommended source is the article of Hoppensteadt (2006). In that article, the models of the ecosystems with species that evolve, compete and seek resources are discussed.

The ABM model permits to include features that can hardly be described by differential equations, like the spatial distribution of individuals, the gregarious instinct, fear, limited food, random walk and evolution. The gregarious effect is a phenomenon whereby the rate of uptake of beliefs, ideas, fads and trends increases the more that they have already been adopted by others. Herd mentality influences behaviors, trends, and/or escape from a threat. In our model the effect consists in gathering the information of movement directions from near neighbors, to take decision on the movement. Consult the old classical publications of

McDougall (1926) or Williams (1933), and more recent works of Mangioni (2012),

The Holling–Tanner model plays an important role. Consult Tanner(1975), Gasull et al. (1997) or Zhang (2012). Models used in these papers take into account the maximal predator per capita consumption rate, number of prey necessary to achieve one-half of the maximum growth rate, the number of prey required to support one predator at equilibrium, among others. Observe that the estimation of parameters of such kind maybe rather difficult, treating with a real, ecological system. Most of the works on such extended models are focused on the mathematical issues, like stability, limit cycles or bifurcation. These issues are not the topic of the present paper because we focus rather on the individual behavioral models and not on differential equations. Our point is that not everything that happens in the real world is described by differential equations.

Gras et al. (2009) discuss an individual-based predator-prey model where the agent behavior is modeled by a fuzzy cognitive map. The Gras model is similar to the models presented in this paper. It considers distance to predator or prey, distance to potential breeding partner, distance to food and energy level. Borshchev et al. (2004) discuss the relation between the continuous ordinary differential (ODE) or system dynamics models and the agent-based modeling. The authors point out that that "*Agent Based approach is more general and powerful because it enables to capture more complex structures and dynamics. The other important advantage is that it provides for construction of models in the absence of the knowledge about the global inter-dependencies*." The prey-predator model discussed in that paper considers the behavior related to the "hunger level," movement over a region, time-delay and some other parameters. No issues like fear, herd instinct or competition are considered.

The main assumption of the L-V and other, extended models is that the rate of prey devoured by the predators, is proportional to the product of the prey and predator densities. For the real system, this assumption is questionable because this rate strongly depends on the spatial distribution, clustering, herd instinct, individual ability to escape, and many other parameters that can hardly be taken into account in continuous versions. The agent-based modeling provides the possibility of simulating the spatial distribution of the individuals. In simulations of such kind we can also generate animations and statistics taken over the populations.

Most of the articles on the continuous L-V models contain discussions on the solutions of the equations and their properties shown on phase-space with isoclines and cycles. The mostly discussed problems are the equilibrium and the stability of the fixed points. The topic of the present article is quite different. In this section, simple simulations of the models are described, and some more advanced treatment of the parameter uncertainty is proposed.

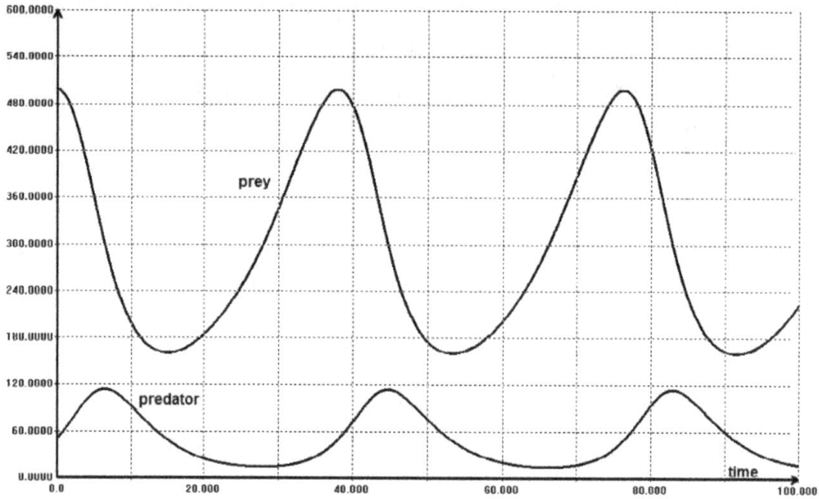

Simple simulation of model (1).

The above figure shows the results of a simple simulation of this model (1). The parameters are fixed, a=0.1, b=0.002, c=0.3, d=0.001. Variable x_1 represents the amount of prey, and x_2 is the amount of predators. The simulation final time is equal to 100 time units. Initial conditions are: prey=500, predator=50. The results show a typical behavior of the model.

The following figure shows the reachable set for the model when the values of parameter a is uncertain and may fluctuate for plus minus 25%(it is a function of time), final time=45. It can be seen that the model has quite big sensitivity with respect to this parameter (as well as the others). The image was obtained using the differential inclusion solver.

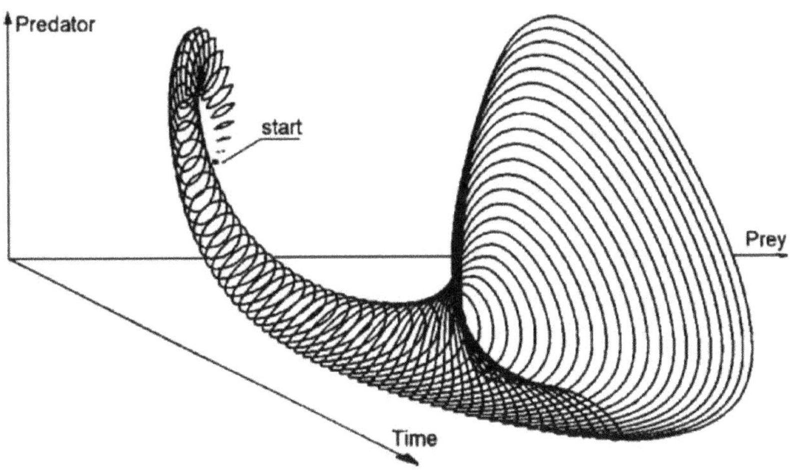

There are many versions of the L-V model, that include the spatial distribution of individuals and multi-species systems, most of them based on the partial differential equations.

The following figure shows an example of a quite complex trajectory of four-species model, plotted on the plane of two species. Most of the models provide the trajectories that hardly reach an equilibrium state. However, they almost always lead to the "orbitally stable" oscillation cycles.

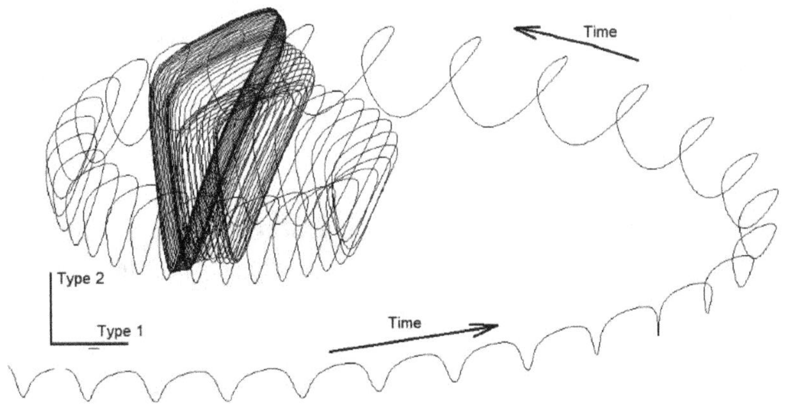

A trajectory of a four-species L-V model.

The Bith/andDeth equation

The *birth-and-death* (B-D) equation may describe the behavior of growing population, queuing systems, communication systems and similar models in probabilistic way. Namely, the solution to the B-D equation is a set of functions of time $P_n(t)$, $n=1,2,3,...N$, where $P_n(t)$ is the probability that the system takes the *n-th* state at the time instant *t*. Note that, though the birth-and death process is a sequence of discrete events and *n* is an integer number, the B-D is a set of ordinary differential equations, and its solution is a set of continuous functions. This occurs because the result describes the probabilities, and not the changes of n.

The total number *N* of possible states is, in most practical cases finite, but in theory it can be infinite. There is an important difference between the experimental frame of the B-D equation model and that of the corresponding model based on discrete events. Modeling, for example, a growth of a population we can create a discrete model (DE) where each event of birth and death of an entity is simulated at a discrete (deterministic or random) time instant. We can also describe the same process by the B-D equation (B-D model). The result of the DE model is a sequence of random events, different for each simulation run. In turn, the result of the B-D model is a sequence of continuous functions $P_n(t)$ that describe *model state probabilities* rather than particular model states. Note that the two corresponding experimental frames are completely different from each other and even do not intersect. One being stochastic and discrete, and the other represented by a deterministic sequence of continuous functions of time.

To obtain the B-D equation of given system, we must define the probability of "birth" (birth of an animal, appearance of call request in a communication system, appearance of a new client in a bank, etc.), and the probability of the "death" or disappearance of a model entity. Then, an assumption is made that the probability that two events occur within a time interval H tends to zero more quickly than the probability that only one event will occur within H, when H approaches zero. This leads to the following equation (the case of population growth):

$$dP_n(t)/dt = -(\lambda_n+\mu_n)P_n(t)+\lambda_{n-1}P_{n-1}(t)+\mu_{n+1}P_{n+1}(t) \quad for \quad n>0,$$
$$dP_0(t)/dt = -\lambda_0 P_0(t)+\mu_1 P_1(t),$$

where λ_n is the birth rate, and μ_n is the death rate if the total population is equal to n.

Both the birth and death rates can depend on the state n, and on the time. For example, in the population model, the birth rate may be proportional to the number of population members, and in a communication system the birth rate is constant or depends on external factors. The number of requests does not depend on how many clients are attended by the system at the moment.

The B-D equation is a useful tool in modeling and simulation. However, in many practical situations it is too primitive to describe the system behavior. Normally, to derive the B-D equation one must first to find how the birth and death rates depend on the system state. This step is frequently the source of errors. For example, while modeling a biological or ecological system the modeler frequently forgets that such systems have a huge and complicated collective memory. Making simple assumptions on the birth and death rates discards this memory and may lead to serious errors.

Marketing model

Marketing is a field where modeling and simulation is of great importance. Unfortunately, market models are charged with big uncertainty. There is a huge number of variables, most of them random or uncertain, what makes the modeling difficult and questionable. The basic marketing model is that describing the demand function. Consult the book:

Kotler P., *Marketing decision making: A model building approach,* Holt-Rinehart-Wilson, 1971, for a great number of demand function models.

The model selection depends on the actual situation and on where and how the model will be used. In general, if the market is stable and no big disturbances are expected, a linear model can be used. This permits to apply linear programming or similar techniques to optimize it. However, if there are big fluctuations in marketing variables and in the environment, we must use a non-linear model. One of the most flexible models is that based on so-called *market elasticities*. An example of such model is as follows.

$$q(p,a,y,v,g,t) = q_0 v(t)s(t)\left(\frac{p(t)}{p(0)}\right)^{e_p}\left(\frac{a(t)}{a(0)v(t)s(t)}\right)^{e_a}\left(\frac{y(t)}{y(0)}\right)^{e_y}$$

where q - demand, q_0 - initial or reference demand,
t - the time, $s(t)$ - overall market size,
$p(t)$ - price, $a(t)$ - advertising per time unit,
$y(t)$ - consumer income, $v(t)$ - seasonal index,
e_p, e_a, e_y - market elasticities with respect to price, advertising and consumer income, respectively. (1)

Normally, the price elasticity is negative (price increase means demand decrease), and the elasticities for advertising and consumer income are positive. The profit can be calculated using the above model as follows

$$U = (1 - b)e - a, \text{ where } e = (p - c)q \qquad (2)$$

U is the profit, and c is the unit cost of the product. This is the simplest profit function. Fixed costs and other factors should be added. The following figure shows the shape of the profit U as a function of the price and advertising, other variables fixed.

It can be seen that the profit function has a maximum that determines the optimal price and advertising.

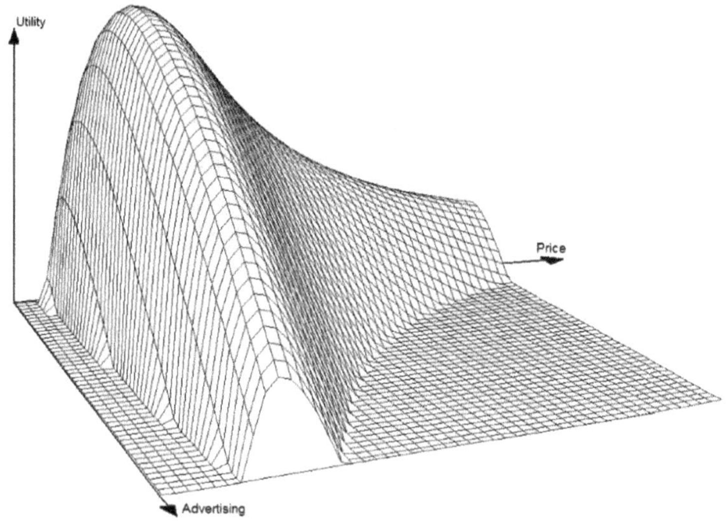

Revenue function

Now, consider a fixed time interval $[0,T]$. To calculate the total revenue, we must integrate (2) over the time. The variable b controls the investment, $0 < b < 1$. The market size growth due to the investment. To make the model more realistic, we suppose that the market growth rate follows the investment with certain inertia. The basic equations are as follows.

$$\begin{cases} \dfrac{dr}{dt} = (1-b)\,v/v_0 \quad \textit{accumulated revenue growth, relative} \\ \textit{where} \quad v = (p-c)\,q(z,w,y,v,s,t) - a, \quad v_0 = \textit{initial revenue} \\ \dfrac{ds}{dt} = (x-s)/T_c \quad \textit{market size growth, relative} \\ \dfrac{dx}{dt} = gbv/v_0 \quad \textit{accumulated investment , relative} \end{cases}$$

This is a non-linear model of the third order. This way, we add some dynamics and inertia to the static model of Kotler.

In the article *Raczynski S., "A Market Model: Uncertainty and Reachable Sets" International Journal for Simulation and Multidisciplinary Design Optimization, EDP Sciences, 2015; 6, (A2), ISBN/ISSN: (Electronic Edition): 1779-6288*, you can find discussion about the reachable sets of this model Here, let us see only an example of the results. The reachable set was obtained supposing that the coefficient b has uncertain value, limited to the interval [0,1], final simulation time 365 days. Consult the article mentioned above for more detail and model specification.

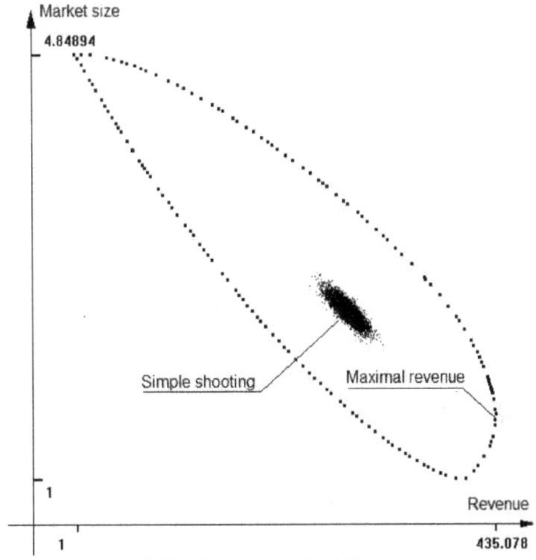

Market reachable set

Epidemics spread

Here, we discuss some properties of the ordinary differential equation (ODE) model of a soft, namely the epidemics model. However, our point is that such model may be invalid, or non-existent. Consult the section "A remark on model existence" for more detail about this issue. Anyway, we comment some properties of the ODE mode.

The Susceptible-Infectious-Removed (SIR) model is a mostly used continuous ODE model of an epidemics. The scheme of the model is shown below. Block S represents the number of susceptible, i.e. the individuals that can be infected. Block I denotes the number of actually infected, R is the number of recovered from the disease with immunity, or dead. A modification of the SIR model named SIRS includes also a feedback from block R to S, as shown below. In the SIRS model it is assumed that some recovered people may be infected again.

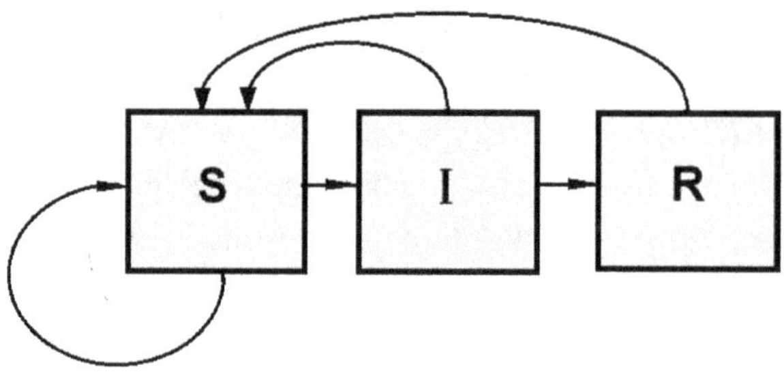

SIRS model

The SIRS model equations are as follows (prime mark stands for time-differentiation).

$$\begin{cases} S' = \dfrac{-\beta SI}{N} + \xi R \\ I' = \dfrac{\beta SI}{N} - \gamma I \\ R' = \gamma I - \xi R \end{cases}$$

In the above, β, ξ and γ are constants. The term ξR represents the number of recovered individuals that return to the S group. The state vector of this model is $X = (S, I, R)$. The following figure shows a typical plot of the S, I and R variables, with $\xi = 0$ (SIR model). The curves are in different scales, they are normalized to the interval [0,1]

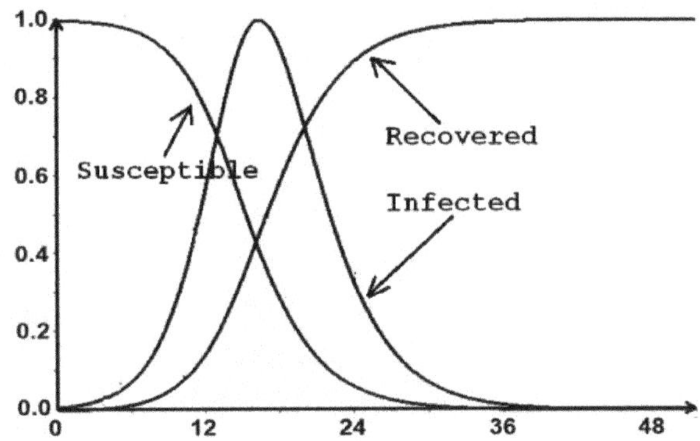

SIR model simulation

The power-series solution to the SIR model is described by Barlow and Weintein (2020). They obtain the long-term solution. The case study of covid-19 is discussed. In the paper of Zheng and Bonasera (2020) there is the discussion of the SIR model solutions compared to the real data. The authors point out that the number of infected, grows exponentially to certain saturation level. The article of Magiarotti et al. (2020) provides a discussion about the governing (ODE) equations and the way to obtain the equations using the available observations. The authors refer to the chaos theory that may be a useful framework while looking for the model equations. An interesting approach, related to the fractal properties of the disease spread is discussed in Tsvetkov et al. (2022). The authors mention some phenomena, difficult to simulate, like the unexpected jumps in the global daily incidence. The presented model is based on differential and integral-differential equations. There are many modifications of the SIR and SIRS models. For epidemics with larger duration, the birth-and-death process is added.

The *passive immunity* is taken into account in the MSIR model, where it is supposed that some individuals are born with the immunity. MSEIR model has the scheme MSEIR, where M is the number of passively immune individuals. Supposing that the immunity in the group R is temporary, we obtain the MSEIRS model. In the article of Ng et al. (2003) we can find a description of a model of double epidemic. The two superimposed epidemics are considered using a modification of the SIR model. The problem is focused on the Hong Kong SARS (Sever Acute Respiratory Syndrome) epidemic in 2003, caused by two different viruses.

The resulting model is given by a system of six differential equations of the first order.

Some more complicated models of epidemic dynamics can be found in Gebreyesus and Chang (2015). They propose a multi-compartment model that takes the interactions of human and animal or different species of animal into account. It is a multivariable state-space model that reflects the phenomena of some diseases transmitted from animal to human, such as Ebola, MERS-Coronavirus bird flu and tuberculosis. The basic model used in that article is a modification of SIR. The main concept is to define a number of clusters in the populations, where the epidemics are governed by SIR equations, interacting with each other. The model supports the spatial issues, introducing the regions like urban and rural. For the models of recurrent epidemics see David and Alla (1994).

It should be noted that the validity of the SIRS model may be questioned. The model does not reflect the following aspect of epidemics:

* Spatial distribution of individuals,
* The shapes of probability density function for incubation period, disease duration and other variables,
* The huge collective memory of soft systems with human factor.

The above deficiencies of the model may suggest that a differential equation model of epidemics may not exist at all. However, in some cases it was pointed out that the SIRS type of model may be useful in epidemic management.

References:

Barlow, N. S. and Weinstein, S. J. (2020). Accurate closed-form solution of the SIR epidemic model. Physica D, 408, 132540. https://doi.org/10.1016/j.physd.2020.132540

David, R. and Alla, H. (1994) Petri nets for modeling of dynamic systems: A survey. Automatica, 30(2), Elsevier, DOI:https://doi.org/10.1016/0005-1098(94)90024-8

Gebreyesus K.D., Chang C.H. (2015) Infectious Diseases Dynamics and Complexity: Multicompartment and Multivariate State-Space Modeling. Conference paper: Proceedings of the World Congress on Engineering and Computer Science 2015

Ng T.W., Turinici G., Danchin A. (2003) A double epidemic model for the SARS propagation. Journal of negative results in biomedicine , BioMed Central, 3(19), DOI: 10.1186/1471-2334-3-19 .

Magiarotti, S., Peyer, M., Zhang, Y., Huc, M., Roger, F. and Kerr, Y. (2020). Chaos theory applied to the outbreak of COVID-19: An ancillary approach to decision making in pandemic context. Epidemiology and Infection, 148, e95, https://doi.org/10.1017/s0950268820000990

Tsvetkov V.P., Mikheev S.A., Tsvetkov I.V., Derbov V.L, Gusev A.A., S.I. and Vinitsky S.I. (2022) Modeling the multifractal dynamics of COVID-19 pandemic, Chaos, Solitons & Fractals, vol 161,https://doi.org/10.1016/j.chaos.2022.112301

Zheng, H. and Bonasera, A. (2020). Chaos, percolation and the coronavirus sread: A two-step model. European Physical Journal Plus, 135, 10. Doi: 10.1140/epip/s13360- 020-00811-z

Stiff equations

Stiffness occurs in a problem where there are two or more very different time scales, for example in systems that have very fast and very slow parts interacting with each other. Consider the following set of equations.

$$\frac{dx_1}{dt} = 998x_1 + 1998x_2$$

$$\frac{dx_2}{dt} = -999x_1 - 1999x_2$$

$$x_1(0) = 1, \ \ x_2(0) = 0$$

The solution is

$$x_1 = 2e^{-t} - e^{-1000t}$$

$$x_2 = -e^{-t} + e^{-1000t}$$

To integrate this system of equations we must define the step size for any numerical methods. For $h<<0.001$ the method normally is stable. However, the term disappears very quickly when t grows. One could suppose that for t between, say 0.1 and 1 we could apply greater integration step because the fast term does not influence the solution. Unfortunately, it is not the case because the integration process becomes unstable even if this term is negligible. This problem is called *stiffness* and it provokes serious difficulties in system simulation.

The most popular methods for stiff equations are:

* Generalizations of the Runge-Kutta method, of which the most useful are the Rosenbrock methods, and their implementation by Kaps-Rentrop.
* Generalization of the Burlisch-Stoer method, due to Bader and Deufhard..
* Predictor-corrector methods

Consult

Kaps P. and Rentrop P., Numerishe Mathematik, vol 33, pp. 55-68, 1979
Bader G and Deufhard P., Numerishe Mathematik, vol 41, pp. 373-398, 1983
Lambert J.D., *Safe point methods for separably stiff systems of ordinary differential equations,* SIAM Journal on Numerical Analysis, 18, 1981, pp. 83-101.

System Dynamics

System Dynamics (SD) is a method for studying the world around us.

The modeled system can be anything from a steam engine, to a bank account, to a basketball team. The objects and people in a system interact through "feedback" loops, where a change in one variable affects other variables over time. This, in turn, affects the original variable, and so on.

System dynamics is a computer-aided approach to policy analysis and design. With origins in servomechanisms and management, the approach uses a perspective based on information feedback and mutual or recursive causality. This helps us understand the dynamics of complex physical, biological, and social systems. With SD we can understand the basic structure of a system and thus, understand the behavior it can produce. Models of many of systems and problems which are analyzed, can be built on a computer. SD takes advantage of the fact that a computer model can be of much great complexity and carry out very fast calculations.

Over the past decades, SD has been applied broadly in such areas as environmental change, economic development, social unrest, urban decay, psychology and physiology.

Jay W. Forrester (http://web.mit.edu/sloan/www/faculty/forrester.html), the creator of System Dynamics, defines it as follows.

Unlike other scientists, who study the world by breaking it up into smaller and smaller pieces, system dynamicists look at things as a whole. The central concept to system dynamics is understanding how all the objects in a system interact with one another. A system can be anything from a steam engine, to a bank account, to a basketball team. The objects and people in a system interact through "feedback" loops, where a change in one variable affects other variables over time, which in turn affects the original variable, and so on.

The seminal book of Jay Forrester *Industrial Dynamics* (1961) is still a significant statement of philosophy and methodology in the field. Since its publication, the span of applications has grown extensively and now encompasses work in

- corporate planning and policy design
- public management and policy
- biological and medical modeling
- energy and the environment
- theory development in the natural and social sciences
- dynamic decision making
- complex nonlinear dynamics

The *System Dynamics Society (SDS)* is an international nonprofit organization devoted to encouraging the development and use of system thinking and system dynamics around the world. With members in fifty-five countries, the Society provides a forum in which researchers, educators, consultants, practitioners in the corporate and public sectors interact.

The SD software and model building are described in section "Software Tools."

See also DYNAMO, STELLA

Electric Circuit Simulation

The Simulation Program with Integrated Circuit Emphasis (SPICE) is a general-purpose electronic circuit simulation tool. A similar, and commonly used and perhaps much user-friendly package is the CircuitMaker. Circuit simulation packages solve the circuits in the static mode (DC current), perform the dynamic analysis using ordinary differential equations (transient processes), and provide the frequency response analysis. Other features like circuit optimization and sensitivity are also available.

SPICE was developed at the University of California at Berkeley and released in 1972. After this, several enhancements have served to eliminate the long-standing claims that SPICE is unfriendly and difficult to use.

Those features are:

* Schematic capture - The process of entering a circuit description into a computer by drawing a picture of the circuit.
* Monte Carlo analysis - The evaluation of circuit performance based on the statistical deviations of parameter tolerances.
* Circuit optimization - The ability to automatically select parameter values based on analysis and a particular circuit performance specification.
* Worst case - The finding and reporting of circuit parameter value(s) which will cause the poorest circuit performance based on some operational criteria.
* Parameter sweeping - The process of changing a given parameter's value over a user specified range and evaluating circuit performance as the parameter varied.
* Parameter extraction hardware and software - Tools used to develop SPICE model parameters for use in simulation.
* Graphics output and post processing - Process of reading SPICE output files to perform analysis operations on the output data. Operations such as integration, differentiation, fast Fourier transform, algebraic waveform manipulation, filtering, and other measurements of the voltage and current are included.

There are several analysis types supported by Spice. The basic ones are the direct current analysis, transient response and frequency response.

Direct current analysis provides a steady-state (static) solution of the simulated network. This analysis is performed always before starting other types of simulations.

In the *transient response mode* SPICE simulates the circuit and displays the transient processes. The circuit components may be linear or non-linear and the simulation is performed with the highest possible accuracy.

In the *frequency response analysis*, the circuit is first resolved in the DC mode. Then, all non-linear elements are linearized in the neighborhood of the DC operation point. Once the model becomes linear, the state transition matrix is calculated and the frequency analysis performed. The results are presented in the form of the Body plots.

SPICE has huge libraries with thousands of models of electronic devices (diodes, transistors, ICs, SCRs, TRIACs etc.) stored together with their parameters.

Partial Differential Equations

We will not discuss the numerical methods for partial differential equations (PDEs). Let us give only some remarks about the difficulties in integrating the equations and the stability of numerical solutions.

Solution algorithms

Partial differential equations (PDE) describe the dynamics of some media, like gas, liquid, or temperature distribution in time and space. To see how complex the problem may be, consider, for example, the following equations of fluid dynamics (Navier– Stokes equations). Here, vector $\boldsymbol{v}$ $=(u,v,w)$ is the velocity of the medium in a point of three-dimensional space with coordinates (x,y,z), and t represents the time (case of liquid flow)

$$\begin{cases} \rho\left(\dfrac{\partial u}{\partial t}+u\dfrac{\partial u}{\partial x}+v\dfrac{\partial u}{\partial y}+w\dfrac{\partial u}{\partial z}\right)=-\dfrac{\partial p}{\partial x}+\mu\nabla^2 u+\rho f_x \\ \rho\left(\dfrac{\partial v}{\partial t}+u\dfrac{\partial v}{\partial x}+v\dfrac{\partial v}{\partial y}+w\dfrac{\partial u}{\partial z}\right)=-\dfrac{\partial p}{\partial y}+\mu\nabla^2 v+\rho f_y \\ \rho\left(\dfrac{\partial w}{\partial t}+u\dfrac{\partial w}{\partial x}+v\dfrac{\partial w}{\partial y}+w\dfrac{\partial w}{\partial z}\right)=-\dfrac{\partial p}{\partial z}+\mu\nabla^2 w+\rho f_z \\ \dfrac{\partial u}{\partial x}+\dfrac{\partial v}{\partial y}+\dfrac{\partial w}{\partial z}=0, \\ where\ \nabla^2=\left(\dfrac{\partial^2}{\partial x^2},\dfrac{\partial^2}{\partial y^2},\dfrac{\partial^2}{\partial z^2}\right) \end{cases} \tag{1}$$

Here, ρ is the liquid density, μ is the viscosity, p is the pressure, and f represented the eventual external force. The above Navier–Stokes equation is difficult to solve, mainly because of its non-linearity and the number of equations. We have three velocity variables and the pressure. Here, the density is supposed constant and we do not deal with the temperature distribution. This means that, after space discretization, we must solve a set of 4N non-linear equations, where N is the number of the grid points, normally between 50,000 and 1,000,000, which gives up to 4,000,000 equations. These difficulties are related to the lack of compressibility of the liquid. In the gas case, we have (in vectorial form):

$$\begin{cases} \dfrac{\partial p}{\partial t} + \nabla \cdot (\rho \mathbf{v}) = 0 \\ \rho \dfrac{\partial v}{\partial t} + \rho \mathbf{v} \cdot \nabla)\mathbf{v} = \nabla \mathbf{p} \\ \rho \dfrac{\partial e}{\partial t} + \rho(v \cdot \nabla)e = -p\nabla \cdot v + \nabla \cdot (k\nabla T) \\ where\, \nabla = \left(\dfrac{\partial}{\partial x}, \dfrac{\partial}{\partial y}, \dfrac{\partial}{\partial z}\right) \end{cases}$$

Here, e is the gas internal energy, ρ is the gas density, T is the temperature, $dT = de/C$, C—specific heat. There is a huge literature that describes a great number of numerical methods for the PDEs. In the book of Ames (1983) *Numerical methods for partial differential equations, 2nd edn., Academic Press, New York*, we can find a good overview of these methods. While solving PDEs, the main difficulties are the computer time and the stability of the numerical method. Most methods use a certain discretization scheme, both in time and space. The problems arise when we decrease the discretization steps to achieve desired time-space resolution. Observe that the PDEs manage time and space differentiation, given by differential operators. The problem is that these *operators are usually unbounded* on the unit sphere in the space of functions. This is the main cause of *numerical instability*.

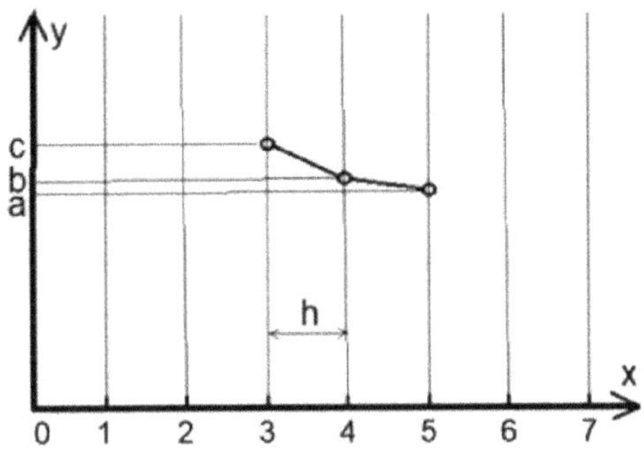

Differentiation scheme

For example, the equations (1) can be rearranged in such a way that we have the time derivative at the left hand and a differential operator on the right. Consider another very simple example. Let y be the dependent variable which changes in time depend on its derivative with respect to space variable x (see Fig. Differentiation scheme). To calculate the increment of y over a consecutive time-step, we must execute the differentiation operation over the space-step of variable x. So, we can use a finite step differencing scheme. The simplest are forward- and backward-differencing that provide the value of the derivative, as follows.

$$d_1 = (y_{n+1} - y_n)/h \text{ and } d_2 = (y_n - y_{n-1})/h, \text{ where } y_n = y(x_n).$$

The problem is, which one of the values d_1 and d_2 should be used? A logical solution seems to be the use of the average $(d_1 + d_2)/2$. This average provides the value

$$D_n=(y_{n+1}-y_{n-1})(2h) \qquad (2)$$

This is called Forward Time-Centered Space (FCTS) scheme. Here, d_n is the estimate of the derivative at x_n. Consequently, we have

$$y_nt + \delta t = y_n(t) + hd_n.$$

Now, observe that the increment of y_n depends on y_{n+1} and y_{n-1} and does not depend on y_n. Thus, the solution for y in the even space-steps depends on the values at odd steps and vice versa. This may result in solutions where y at even and odd space points are quite different. This fact shows how useless is the FTCS differencing scheme. Moreover, it is known that integration with this differencing scheme is *always unstable*. The common remedy to the FTCS instability is the LAX method (see Lax PD, Wendroff

B (1960) Systems of conservation laws. Commun Pure Appl Math 13(2):217–237. https://doi.org/10.1002/cpa.3160130205). In this method, we replace Eq. (2) with the following.

$$d = (y_{n+1} - y_{n-1})/(2h) - v\_t\ 2h\ (d_{n+1} - d_{n-1}). \quad (3)$$

The last term of (3) stabilizes the scheme. Here, v is a constant, sometimes called wave propagation speed, and $\_t$ is the time-step. The LAX method, however, is not any "magic" remedy for the PDE solution. In general, the use of (3) is equivalent to adding some artificial viscosity or dissipation, to the solution. This results in stable solutions but by adding a dissipation to the model we, in fact, solve an altered problem. There are a lot of other methods that make the differencing schemes stable. Unfortunately, these methods almost always alternate the original model.Another inconvenience is that the increase of the time–space resolution results in a rapid increment of the computing time. Better results are obtained by the *finite element method*, shortly described in the following

Finite element method

The main difference between finite step differencing algorithms and the *finite element method* is that the space discretization is not uniform. A *mesh* of small *finite elements* is defined. The elements need not be cubes. They are rather volume elements with different sizes and shapes that fill the volume under consideration. Depending on the physical properties of the medium (gas, liquid, heat, electromagnetic field, etc.), the algebraic equation for the finite element is defined. This leads to the problem of solution to a number of algebraic equations, solved by the methods of the calculus of variations and optimization. The main software tool for finite element method is the ANSYS package, equipped with a sophisticated numerical algorithm, graphical user interface, and 3D results display. We will not discuss here the details of the finite element method because the topic of this book is not the numerical analysis, but rather general concepts of model building. For more detail, consult [3, 10, 27].

Example: Jet takeoff vibrations

In many occasions, passengers complain about the strong vibrations of the fuselage during the plane lift-off. This makes the takeoff unpleasant. One of the causes of vibrations may be the air turbulence below the wing. This can be simulated by solving the Navier–Stokes equations. Let's show here only the most relevant result. Below figure shows the velocity field around the wing just after takeoff. This is a two-dimensional projection of the three-dimensional simulation. On the animated simulation screen, it can be seen that around the wing big vibrations and turbulence appear that generate the vibrations in air pressure. This results in strong vibrations of the whole fuselage and may even be dangerous for the structure of the fuselage. The model and simulation experiments have been done using the Fluids6 simulation program. The simulations of this, and similar models show that the fluid flow hardly reaches a steady state. Such a state may satisfy the fluid equations, but in reality, never takes place. So, many of the results provided by the fluid dynamics software may be correct from the mathematical point of view, but useless and confusing in design tasks because the velocity field is always in movement. The above modeling and simulations are important for safety issues.

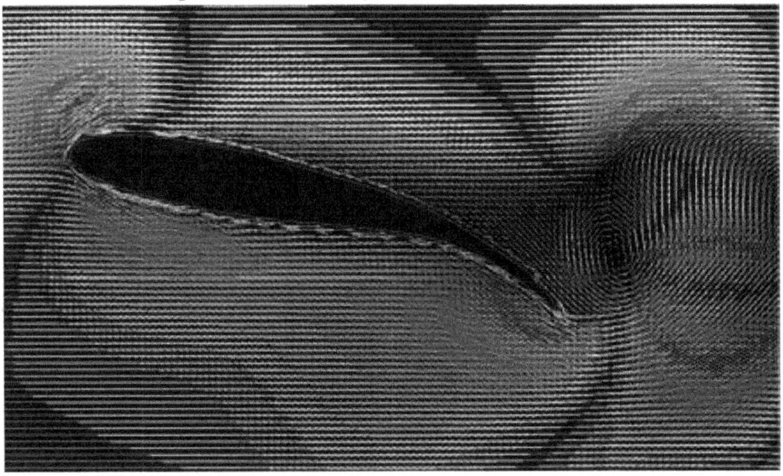

Air flow around the wing. Velocity field.

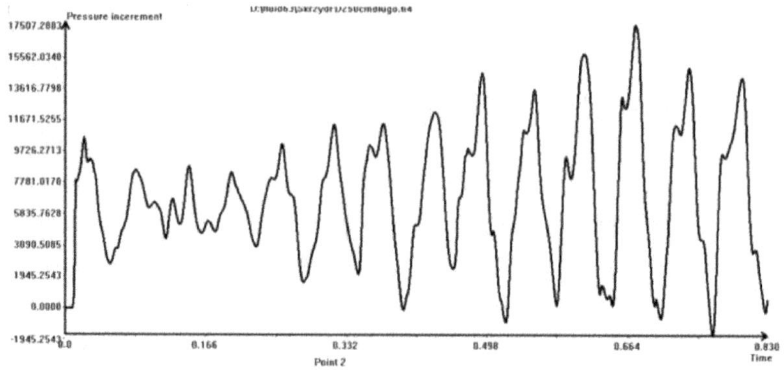

Low-frequency pressure oscillation below the wing.

Chapter 3

Continuous Simulation Software Tools

Below, you can find a list of, perhaps most relevant, software tools for continuous simulation. Some of the packages are obsolete, they are listed for historical reasons.

ACSL

This is a simulation language used for modeling continuous, nonlinear dynamical systems. The design of ACSL goes well beyond full compliance with the Continuous System Simulation Language standard to provide a wide range of modeling and analysis tools. ACSL supports rapid, interactive experimentation as well as batch operation. A graphical-front end for visual programming is available.

acslXtreme is a powerful tool for modeling continuous dynamic systems and processes. Simple to learn, easy to use, acslXtreme is designed to solve today's most demanding scientific problems.

acslXtreme allows you to model the full nonlinear behavior of your system or process. There is no limitation on program size, number of equations, states or variables. So, your model can represent large real-life system with all of the complexities, without impairing your ability to understand, use, describe, and present them to your colleagues.

In the graphic design mode, you have the choice of using off-the-shelf or custom PowerBlocks. You can either create your own model "libraries" or use the extensive set of commonly used mathematical functions and operators provided with acslXtreme.

If you prefer, you can create models using the advanced Continuous Simulation Language (CSL), the industry-standard representation language for continuous systems. In addition, modeling constructs are provided that allow you to model discrete state changes in the continuous system.

The AEgis Technologies Group, Inc.
631 Discovery Drive
Huntsville, AL 35806
Phone: 800-647-2275
Phone: 256-922-0802
Fax: 256-883-5516
Email: sales@AEgisTG.com
Web Site: www.acslX.com

ADAMS

Simulation package that enables engineers to para-metrically model 3D mechanical systems and study alternative designs as "virtual prototypes." ADAMS simulations are used to evaluate system performance, range of motion, collision detection, packaging, peak loads, end FEA input loads. Two-way interfaces with CAD, FEA, and controls design packages are supported.

ADAMS version 10 (Automatic Dynamic Analysis of Mechanical Systems) from Mechanical Dynamics Inc., USA is the world's most widely used software for mechanical system simulation. The ADAMS line of software products can help you improve the design of anything that moves - from simple linkages and small electromechanical devices to complex vehicles, aircraft and machinery. ADAMS operates within a four step process:

Modelling: Within the easy-to-use interface, you can build a mechanical system model by importing data from CAD software or by starting from scratch, using the ADAMS libraries of part shapes, joints, motion generators and forces.

Solution: Will your system function properly, avoiding lock-up positions and interferences with other parts or systems? Will the system movement and performance match specifications? Will the internal force be too high? ADAMS can tell you. It automatically formulates and solves the equations of motion, and computes all displacements, velocities, accelerations and forces.

Visualization: With a click of a button you can examine x-y plots, or view fast, realistic animations superimposed, or in still-frame.

Design Optimization: Change one or more variables, press a button and ADAMS will perform a simulation of the revised model and make comparisons. ADAMS' parametric design simulation capabilities allow you to evaluate an unlimited number of designs, and pinpoint the optimal design - before a single piece of metal is being cut or cast.

To facilitate virtual prototyping process, a number of ADAMS software modules are available:

ADAMS Full Simulation Package: including ADAMS/Solver and ADAMS/View.

ADAMS/Animation: to provide very high-speed, photo-realistic animations.

ADAMS/Car: modelling and analysis of car suspension systems and full vehicle modelling of dynamic ride and handling studies.

ADAMS/Controls: sophisticated controls systems can be developed without writing the mechanical system equations directly.

ADAMS/Driver: simulation of control actions of a vehicle driver such as steering, braking, accelerating, gear shifting, and clutching.

ADAMS/Engine: offers specialized utilities for valve train design and testing of timing mechanisms, belts, cranks, and pistons.

ADAMS/Flex: allows flexible parts to be created within ADAMS models from modal frequency data.

ADAMS/Hydraulics: helps you smoothly integrate system-level motion simulation and hydraulic system design.

ADAMS/Insight: allows you to plan and run a series of experiments for measuring the performance of your mechanical system design in operation.

ADAMS/Linear: linear and eigenvalue analysis, particularly when integrating mechanical simulation with controls design software.

ADAMS/Pre: provides automakers and their suppliers with a suite of specialized pre-processing capabilities to quickly create a complete computer model of a full-vehicle or vehicle-subsystem design.

ADAMS/Rail: modelling and analysis of rail suspension systems and full vehicle modelling of dynamic ride and handling studies.

ADAMS/Tire: accurately predicts the influence of tire characteristics on vehicle operation.

ADAMS/Exchange: automates the exchange of geometry data between ADAMS and CAD systems supporting any of a variety of standards including IGES, DXF, STEP, VDAFS, and STL.

MECHANISM/Pro: is seamlessly integrated within the Pro/ENGINEER environment allowing users to easily convert assemblies created with PTC's Pro/ASSEMBLY software into realistic, fully 3-D mechanical system models by adding joints, forces, and motion generators from MECHANISM/Pro.

CAT/ADAMS: allows quick and easily transfer of CATIA-generated component and system geometry, as well as mechanism data from CATIA Kinematics, to the ADAMS solution engine for dynamic simulation of your complete mechanism in motion.

Contact: Mechanical Dynamics, Inc., 2301 Commonwealth Blvd., Ann Arbor, MI 48105.

ADSIM

ADSIM is a simulation language for writing simulation models, debugging and verifying programs, running experiments, and analyzing and documenting results. Easy to learn and highly interactive, ADSIM enables the user to validate, observe, and manipulate the model without recompiling. ADSIM was specifically developed to provide real-time solutions on a variety of computer engines.

Platform : VAX or SPARK II

Contact: Applied Dynamics International, 3800 Stone School Rd., Ann Arbor, MI 48108.

AcslXtreme of AEGIS

acslXtreme is a powerful tool for modeling continuous dynamic systems and processes. Simple to learn, easy to use, acslXtreme is designed to solve today's most demanding scientific problems. Developed by AEgis. We mention this tool for historical reasons. ACSL and acslXtreme has ended on December 31, 2004.

acslXtreme allows you to model the full nonlinear behavior of your system or process. When modeling systems that involve both controls and physical systems, for example, there is no need to "linearize" the physical system model to be able to design and apply the controller. With acslXtreme, nonlinear system attributes are fully represented. There is no limitation on program size, number of equations, states or variables. So, your models can represent large real-life systems with all of the complexities, without impairing your ability to understand, use, describe, and present them to your colleagues.

In the graphic design mode, you have the choice of using off-the-shelf or custom PowerBlocks. You can either create your own model "libraries" or use the extensive set of commonly used mathematical functions and operators provided with acslXtreme.

If you prefer, you can create models using the advanced Continuous Simulation Language (CSL), the industry-standard representation language for continuous systems. In addition, modeling constructs are provided that allow you to model discrete state changes in the continuous system.

The AEgis Technologies Group, Inc.
631 Discovery Drive
Huntsville, AL 35806
Phone: 800-647-2275
Phone: 256-922-0802
Fax: 256-883-5516
Email: sales@AEgisTG.com
Web Site: www.acslX.com

ALGOR

Finite Element Analysis and Event Simulation Software. It performs 2D and 3D finite element linear static stress analysis on 3D CAD models with Algor's Basic software program. Other features include surface and solid modeling using Algor's geometry/model control center, Superdraw. Both, surface and solid models can be visualized with Algor's animation utility. The program offers complete post processing and CAD interfacing via 2D/3D wire-frame geometry from virtually any CAD system.

Algor's Graduate package combines everything in the Basic package plus weight, center of gravity and a mass moment of inertia processor. This advanced program includes extended surface modeling with Supersurf and Hypergen automatic solid tetrahedral mesh generation for FEA modeling.

All Algor programs include: DocuTech - Software Documentation Information Resource. This CD-ROM contains software and reference documentation, educational materials, keystroke-specific tutorials, and product information that can be accessed through a powerful search utility.

Hardware Requirements: Pentium-based PC, Windows® 95/98/NT 3.51TM, 64 bit color graphics card, 120 MB hard disk space, 32 MB RAM minimum (64 recommended).

Mailing Address:
Tech Ed Concepts, Inc.
550 Pembroke Street
Pembroke, NH 03275 USA
Phone/Fax:
Toll Free: (800) 338-2238 Local: (603) 224-8324
Fax: (603) 225-7766
Email: sales@tecedu.com custservice@tecedu.com

ANSYS

A software package for distributed parameter models. Models of such systems are given in the form of partial differential equations. ANSYS uses the finite element analysis (FEA) to solve given problems. Though the original FEA problems were static and belong rather to engineering and design (CAD), the whole field is supposed to belong to simulation. New FEA applications include also dynamic models, so can be treated as simulation software.

ANSYS/Multiphysics incorporates the full range of ANSYS coupled-field, multiphysics capabilities. It combines structural, thermal, acoustics, piezoelectric, current conduction, circuits, CFD, mechanical, and electromagnetic features in one design analysis software that performs multiple analyses and coupled-field analyses simultaneously.

Direct and indirect (sequential) coupling are two methods of coupled-field analysis available in ANSYS/Multiphysics. Direct coupling involves a single design analysis using coupled-field elements that have multiple degrees of freedom at each node to allow continual cross-coupling between the analytical disciplines. The indirect method involves two sequential design analyses, each belonging to a different field. The two fields are coupled by applying results from the first design analysis as loads for the second design analysis. Each method proves beneficial to different users. With the direct method, it is possible to determine complex acoustics/ structural response or piezoelectric phenomena. Sequential coupling is extremely attractive for coupled-field interactions that are not highly nonlinear.

ANSYS/Multiphysics includes also a computational fluid dynamics (CFD) software, ANSYS/Flotran, and a self-contained electromagnetic analysis package, ANSYS/Emag.

ANSYS/Flotran has the capability of solving a variety of fluid flow problems, including laminar, turbulent, compressible, and incompressible flow; subsonic, transonic, and supersonic; single or multiple fluids. It provides multiphysics capabilities, enabling analysis of the interaction fluid, thermal, and structural phenomena.

ANSYS/Emag contains extensive 2D and 3D analysis capabilities including the simulation of electromagnetic fields, electrostatics, circuits, low and high frequency current conduction. This program, when used with other ANSYS products, generates multiphysics capabilities enabling the study of the interaction of flow, electromagnetic fields, and structural mechanics.

ANSYS includes also a preprocessor and a postprocessor which can be entered through the graphical user interface.

On the CILEA machines is installed also ANSYS/LS-DYNA 5.5. This is a finite element code particularly suited for analyzing non-linear dynamic responses of 3D structures, also coupled with fluids. The computation is based on explicit dynamic solver, but an implicit solver is also available, with limited capabilities. The LS-DYNA program, now included in ANSYS, has been developed from a public domain program named DYNA3D. DYNA3D has been written on 1976 at the Lawrence

Livermore National Laboratory.

Contact: http:/www.ansys.com

AUTOSIM

AUTOSIM is an automatic, discrete event simulation generator developed by the Operations Research Section at the BHP Newcastle Steelworks. It has now been used for a number of years in developing simulation models in an industrial environment. The system to be simulated is first described as an Activity Cycle Diagram (ACD) which is then encoded for input to the AUTOSIM program generator. AUTOSIM, itself a SIMULA program, translates this code together with a number of simulation parameters into a complete working SIMULA program.

Consult: Warren H.I.,Low R.A.., Hughes P.D.. and Gray G.J. (1985) "AUTOSIM: An automatic simulation program generator," Mathematics and Computers in Simulation, vol.27, issue2-3, pp.107-114.

FLOTRAN

Solving a variety of computational fluid dynamics (CFD) problems, ANSYS/FLOTRAN is the very definition of flexible CFD software. Manufacturing companies in industries ranging from automotive, aerospace, and heavy machinery, to computers and electronics use ANSYS/FLOTRAN to produce high-quality designs and reduce costly prototyping cycles.

Whether you need flow coefficients for several candidate valve designs, or an understanding of the sheer stresses in blood flow through a microfluidic "lab-on-a-chip," ANSYS/FLOTRAN can help you evaluate the design concepts and optimize your final choice. With automated, unstructured meshing, advanced turbulence models, solid numerics, and informative graphics, ANSYS/FLOTRAN is the price/performance leader in CFD simulation.

Contact: ANSYS, Inc.
Southpointe
275 Technology Drive
Canonsburg, PA 15317
http://www.ansys.com

CADSIM

Dynamic Chemical Process Simulation Software. CADSIM Plus is an easy-to-use, fully self-contained, process simulation platform which allows the user to quickly draw a process flowsheet drawing - and create a process simulation - all at the same time. It is a single tool that can both balance flowsheets and portray dynamic conditions.

CADSIM Plus performs precise heat and material balances of any chemical process. It can be used for design, to find solutions for process bottlenecks, to track potential quality control problems, to refine process waste management strategies, to improve process efficiencies, to train and more.

Hardware Requirements: Any personal computer with a high-resolution display suited to CAD.

Software Requirements: Windows 95, 98, NT, 2000

Training Requirements: Chemical process engineering skills.

CONTACT: Aurel Systems Inc, mail@aurelsystems.com

CSSL

A simulation software system designed to assist engineers to and scientists to mathematically model dynamic systems and to interactively conduct experiments on these models. This allow us in order to gain insight into the model behavior. CSSL-IV is a version of CSSL that includes a complete simulation environment that facilitates rapid model definition, accurate experimentation, and graphic display of data.

CSSL IV provides advanced tools for nonlinear optimization, stiff equations integration, frequency response, spectral analysis and linear algebra. It also supports bond-graph front end.

Platform: Apollo, CDC, DEC, HP, UNISYS, PC.

Contact: Simulation Service International, 9414 Irondale Avenue Chatsworth, CA 91311

DADS

Dynamic Analysis and Design System (DADS) is a mechanical computer-aided engineering (MCAE) software package that enables the simulation and analysis of mechanisms and complex mechanical systems. DADS Revision 7.0 delivers motion analysis and simulation capabilities in a unified, interactive user environment.

Platform: Alliant, CDC, Convex, CRAY, DEC, Fujitsu, HP/Aplollo, IBM, Silican Graphics, SUN, Solbourne.

Contact: CADSI 2651 Crosspark Road, Coralville, IA 52241

DSNP

Dynamic Simulator for Nuclear Power Plants. It is a simulation language with special application for the dynamic analysis of nuclear power plants. It is used to simulate transients in any nuclear system for design, safety and operational purposes.

Platform: PC, UNIX, VAX, requires Fortran 77.

Contact: System Simulation and Analysis, POBox 199, Western Springs, IL 60558.

DYMOLA

This is a symbolic formula manipulation system that assembles the equations from sub-models, adds the appropriate connection equations, and then transforms the equations to the form suitable for the simulation system. DYMOLA can generate code for a variety of simulation languages including ACSL, SimuLink, Desire, and few more. It can also directly generate either Fortran or C code.

The DYMOLA system contains also the following tools.

Dymodraw - a graphical general-purpose object diagram editor that enables the user to compose models of systems from models of subsystems topologically connecting them. The end product of the graphical model is a textual model encoded in DYMOLA.

Dymosim - a C-based continuous-time simulation system. It supports both differential and differential-algebraic equations.

Dymoview - a graphical post processor that provides plotting of simulation results as well as 3D postanimation of mechanical systems.

Contact: Dr Francois E. Cellier, Electric and Computer Engineering Dept., The University of Arizona, USA.

DYNAMO

A simulation language based on the method of J.Forrester that implements main concepts of System Dynamics. Accepts model expressed in the form of ordinary differential equation or difference equations. The model is described in terms of flows and levels. The levels are integrals of the total flows affecting the level. The flows can be controlled by algebraic functions of the model state (the levels), so any complex feedback system can be simulated.

In models of organizations, there are defined flows of information, material, orders, working power, capital, funds etc. The corresponding levels represent the actual state of the organization.

Used for models of economic systems, organizations, urban development and similar.

See also : STELLA

EASYx

A package sed to model non-linear dynamic and sampled-data systems, perform simulations, steady-state analyses, analyze/design control systems, perform data analysis, generate/sort source code, and perform real-time hardware-in-loop simulation. GUI-based. Non-linearities and stiff systems model with Switch States simulated.

Platform: SUN, HP, HP/Apollo, DEC, SGI, IBM RS6000.

Contact: Boeing, POBox 24346 M/S 7L-23, Seattle, WA 98124-0346

ECOSIM Pro

EcosimPro is a state-of-the-art, continuous simulation tool. It is an open tool. Firstly, it is not domain-specific and libraries have already been developed for several domains. Moreover, it can easily be extended by the user, and there are no strange rules to write subroutines in FORTRAN or C.

It can be used to study both the transient behavior and the steady state of models, and also to linearize the model behavior around a working point.

EcosimPro has a good graphical interface which facilitates the modeling task. Icons appearing in the model editor correspond to the real components of your system. In EcosimPro, What You Draw Is What You

Model (Wydiwym). Very few simulation tools really offer this capability, although to judge from their commercial literature you might well think the opposite.

EcosimPro as originally developed by EA for the European Space Agency (ESA). It started in 1989, and at present it is available in version 3.0 for Windows NT,95 and 98 platforms.

EcosimPro has been applied in industry. A number of companies mainly in the aerospace sector, ESTEC, DORNIER and CEA, to name but a few, have used the tool. The original purpose of EcosimPro was to model Environment Control and Life Support Systems (ECLSS) for HERMES and COLUMBUS.

There are therefore well-tested libraries of components for ECLSS, such as cabin pressure regulation, temperature and humidity control, etc. Since then, many other components and libraries have been developed for fields other than ECLSS: thermohydraulics, control components, fuel cells, propulsion, flight mechanics, missiles and guided weapons, electrical circuits, attitude and orbit control systems (AOCS), power plants, etc.

Contact: Empresarios Agrupados address:
c/ Magallanes, 3
28015 Madrid
Spain
Tlf : 34 - 1 - 309 8000 Fax : 34 - 1 - 445 0113

ESL

ESL is a new Continuous System Simulation Language (CSSL) which is being developed under contract from the European Space Agency. (European Space Agency Simulation Language). It is an advances continuous systems simulation software environment, provides two user interfaces: high-level language, or mouse driven block diagram form of simulation specification. An interpreter provides fast turn-around for program development. Post-mortem graphic analysis is performed by the DISP (graphics display) system.

Platform: PC DOS/Windows, UNIX, SUN, HP, Silicon, IBM RS6000, DEC, VMS and ULTRIX.

Contact: ISIM International Simulation Ltd., Technology House

Salford University Business Park, Lissadel Street, Salford M66AP, England.

https://doi.org/10.1177/003754978504400505

FANSIM

Analysis and synthesis of time series or transient response by Fast Fourier Transform techniques. Frequency response as Bode plots, Nyquist plots or filed spectral data. Poles, zeros and/or transfer functions as well as enhanced graphical output module and printing utilities for presentations are supported.

Contact: TUTSIM Products, 200 California Ave. 212, Palo Alto, CA 94306.

FLUIDS6

FLUIDS6 solves the Navier-Stokes (N-S) equation for an incompressible fluid that flows through 3D channels with obstacles. The channel and the obstacles can be arbitrary 3D shapes. Optionally, the channel may be axisymmetric.

Recall that the N-S equation is a nonlinear partial equation that describes fluid dynamics. The N-S equation is complemented by the continuity equation. The whole system represents a set of nonlinear partial differential equations with four unknown variables assigned to each point of the 3D region: the pressure and the three components of the particle velocity.

The algorithm implemented in this program was designed to find a steady solution for the N-S equation. Unfortunately, there are situations in which such solution does not exist. When the Reynolds number of the real flow is high or when the channel shape is complicated (including very narrow "bottlenecks"), the strong turbulence may occur and the algorithm does not converge.

The flow is considered to occur in an axi-symmetric or irregular channel that has an inlet and outlet. However, the user can define any other configuration, like, for example, an open region where some internal points have fixed pressure, being sources of the flow. The boundary conditions are defined as sets of points with fixed pressure and fixed velocity. It is supposed that the velocity on all solid boundaries is equal to zero. The pressure at all inlet/outlet points must be defined by the user and remains fixed.

FLUIDS6 program includes a 3D channel editor. The channel shape is defined graphically. For the axisymmetric channel the user draws the channel projection. For the arbitrary channel the shape is defined by sections (layers) on the X-Y plane that are given consecutive Z coordinate values. Then, the program creates the set of grid points to discretize the problem in space. A normal channel needs about 200,000 points, so that the total amount of unknown variables is about 800,000 (the pressure and the three velocity components for each point).

The FLUIDS6 display screens show the 3D or 2D channel and obstacles images with variable view angles. The following result images are provides.

** Velocity in a vertical (Y-Z), horizontal (X-Z) or X-Y projections. The velocity is marked at each grid point as a section which direction shows the particle velocity direction. The length of the velocity indicator may be constant or proportional to the absolute velocity, and the color changes with the velocity.

** Pressure marked at each point with a corresponding color

** Rotation marked with a corresponding color. The rotation is the sum of the absolute values of the components of the rotation tensor

** Flow lines in X-Z, Y-Z and X-Y projections

Example

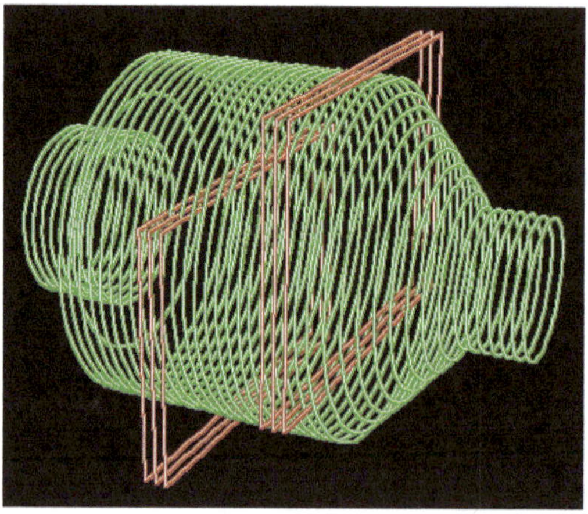

This image shows an axisymmetric channel with two rectangular obstacles. The left and right ends of the channel are open. The pressure on the left end (inlet) if fixed to 20 N/(sqr m) and the pressure at the right end (outlet) is equal to zero. It is supposed that the liquid that flows through the channel is water at 22 centigrade. The solution shown at the following figures needs about 20 minutes of computing time on a 200 MHz PC.

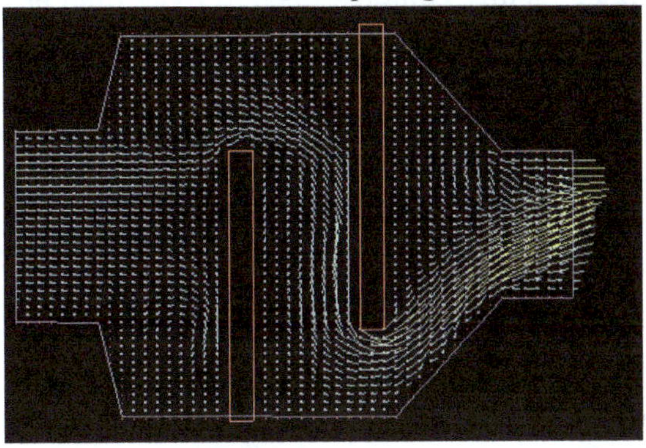

The above figure shows the velocity distribution in the Y-Z projection (a section of the channel with a vertical plane X=0). The length of the velocity sections is proportional to the velocity. The velocity is also marked with different colors: blue sections represent low velocity, while the yellow means big velocity.

The following images shows the flow lines in vertical and horizontal intersections

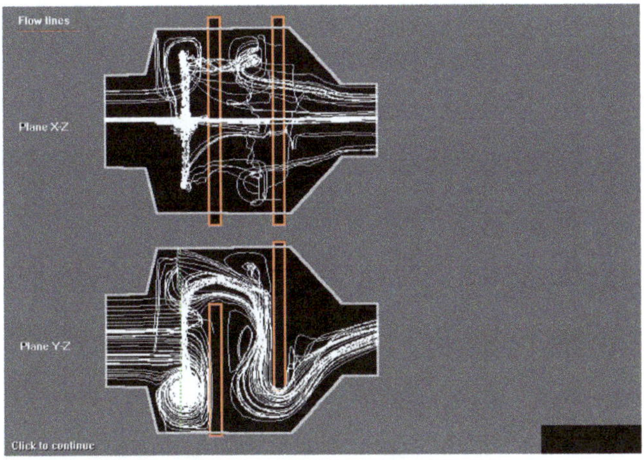

Contact: stanracz@gmail.com

PIPESIM

General purpose multiphase flow simulation software for wells and pipeline systems

PIPESIM for Windows is a general purpose multiphase flow simulator for wells, flowlines and pipeline systems including surface equipment (e.g. chokes, separators, pumps, compressors, etc.) The fluid properties can be modelled via black-oil correlations or fully compositional. A wide choice of industry standard multiphase flow correlations are available including the mechanistic models of Ansari, Xiao and OLGA-S. PIPESIM for Windows offers users the rigorous modelling of oil, gas and condensate multiphase flows.

Provider: Baker Jardine & Associates Ltd

info@bjalondon.com

POWERSIM

POWERSIM software helps users to **develop** business models, to **analyze** and **tune** the models, and to **distribute** the simulations to end users on CD-ROM or over the web.

POWERSIM Constructor is used for creating system-dynamics models that are the heart of a business simulator. This software allows you to create diagrams that represent a system, such as your department, factory, or company, and develop the diagram into an interactive dynamic model.

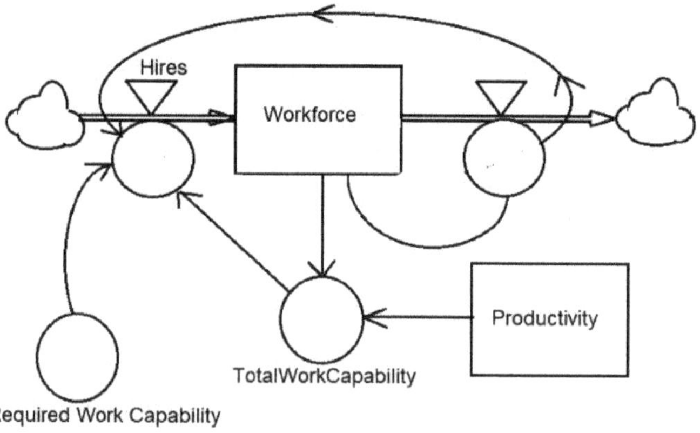

You begin by creating a diagram or model of your problem or your organization, then add mathematical formulas to each element in the diagram. You create the diagram by using a small set of basic building blocks of which the most important are stocks and flows. A stock represents a pool of materials, people, money, or other resources. A flow represents the activities that increase or decreases the stock.

By linking the stock to the flow, you can model a feedback loop that describes how managers, employees, and customers make decisions based on information they see in their daily environment. Simulate this model and you will see graphs and tables showing how these decisions and assumptions play out over time.

In addition to incorporating this powerful modeling methodology, Constructor includes many other features that can help you build large, sophisticated models of your business problem. These include:

Large Function LibraryAdd power to your model with over 150 specialized functions including financial, mathematical, statistical, and delay functions.

Graphical FunctionsModel non-linear or imprecise relationships by drawing the relationship in a graph instead of entering an algebraic equation.

DDEConnect to Excel and other applications through Dynamic Data Exchange.

ArraysReplicate model structures by segmenting your model into multiple competitors, products, vendors, and/or market segments.

Co-ModelsPartition a model into separate files assisting team members in working independently.

Powersim software can be connected to other databases in several different ways:

API: Application Programming Interface that lets other programs access Powersim.

DDE: Dynamic Data Exchange, which is a standard Windows approach to data exchange between applications. Using the DDE transfer object, Powersim acts as a DDE client, sending and receiving data. Powersim may also act as a DDE server, allowing other applications to start and control Powersim using DDE commands.

OLE: Object Linking and Embedding. This feature allows other software programs to control Powersim. For example, a Powersim diagram may be included in an Excel spreadsheet document.

Platform: Powersim tools are Windows 95,98 and NT 3.5,4.0 and 5.0 compatible. Powersim tools can also run as a server on an NT machine, and have JAVA clients running the simulation over Intranet or Internet. The only requirement for the clients is that they need a JAVA enabled browser, or a Java Virtual Machine (JVM) installed, which means that the clients can be run on any platform that has a JVM.

Contact: Powersim Corporation
1175 Herndon Parkway, Suite 600
Herndon, VA 20170
(703) 481-1270
powersim@powersim.com

PROENGINEER

The Pro/ENGINEER® Mechanism Design Extension enables designers to assemble Pro/ENGINEER parts and sub-assemblies using pre-defined connections (pin joints, ball joints, sliders, etc.) to create a mechanism assembly. These connections are intelligent Pro/ENGINEER features and can be used in conjunction (and are interchangeable with) the traditional assembly constraints like mate, align and insert. The mechanism can then be interactively dragged through its range of motion, or by using ‘drivers,’ animations of pre-defined motion can be created, stored and replayed.

One of the most important ideas of ProEngineer is the way mechanisms are created and documented. In the traditional approach, the designed expressed his ideas in the form of 2D technical drawings and the 3D view has been the result of the design process. In the new versions of ProEngineer this design mode is reversed: first, the designer creates the 3D object, revises its features such as 3D movement of the parts, and then generates 2D drawings as a secondary design documentation.

Capabilities

Concurrent design and simulation

Mechanisms are created, edited and moved using tools available to the Pro/ENGINEER user through the 'Designed for Windows®' user interface. The mechanisms are assembled and manipulated directly in Pro/ENGINEER, so there's no data transfer problems to worry about and users get the benefits of true associativity and interoperability with other PTC products and data management tools.

Interactive mechanism manipulation

The ability to interactively drag any point or part in a mechanism assembly to see how the mechanism operates provides designers with early insight into design performance and brings the real-world behavior of their product into the virtual environment of Pro/ENGINEER. A library of powerful 'drivers' is available to generate animations where pre-defined movements are required.

Behavioral Modeler integration

Pro/ENGINEER users can use behavioral modeling functionality to perform design optimization studies of mechanism behavior to quickly arrive at design solutions which previously took multiple time-consuming iterations to calculate.

Swept volume envelope

In many cases, designers need to know the maximum extent of movement of a mechanism when moving through a series of motions. Pro/ENGINEER can calculate and store this swept volume as a real part which can then be used or exported for space-claim purposes or other design studies.

Interference and clash detection

Mechanism Design automatically detects and calculates volumetric interference between any interfering parts, so that costly re-design downstream can be avoided.

Design intent re-use

The mechanism joints in Mechanism Design are re-used by Pro/MECHANICA® when dynamic mechanism simulation is required and by the Design Animation Option module where they can be selectively activated during the animation sequences.

Contact:

PTC

128 Technology Drive
Waltham, MA 02453
USA
Phone: 781-398-5000

SIMULINK

A software package for continuous simulation of dynamic systems represented by block diagrams. Simulink is a part of the Matlab software family.

The model is created by dragging block icons into the screen. No written code needed. More than 200 built-in block types are provided. The user can also design his own blocks with custom icons. Principal applications: control systems, signal processing.

Platform: PC Windows, Macintosh.

Contact: Math Works, Inc., 24 Prime Park Way/Natick, MA 017560.

SPICE

The Simulation Program with Integrated Circuit Emphasis (SPICE) is a general-purpose electronic circuit simulation tool. SPICE was developed at the University of California at Berkeley and released in 1972. After this, several enhancements have served to eliminate the long-standing claims that SPICE is unfriendly and difficult to use. Those are:

* Schematic capture - The process of entering a circuit description into a computer by drawing a picture of the circuit.
* Monte Carlo analysis - The evaluation of circuit performance based on the statistical deviations of parameter tolerances.
* Circuit optimization - The ability to automatically select parameter values based on analysis findings and a particular circuit performance specification.
* Worst case - The finding and reporting of circuit parameter value(s) which will cause the poorest circuit performance based on some operational criteria.
* Parameter sweeping - The process of changing a given parameter's value over a user specified range and evaluating circuit performance

as the parameter varied.

* Parameter extraction hardware and software - Tools used to develop SPICE model parameters for use in simulation.
* Graphics output and post processing - Process of reading SPICE output files to perform analysis operations on the output data. Operations such as integration, differentiation, fast Fourier transform, algebraic waveform manipulation, filtering, and other measurements of the voltage and current are included.

There are several analysis types supported by Spice. The basic ones are the direct current analysis, transient response and frequency response.

The direct current analysis provides a steady-state (static) solution of the simulated network. This analysis is performed always before starting simulations of another type.

In the transient response mode SPICE simulates the circuit and displays the transient processes. The circuit components may be linear or non-linear and the simulation is performed with the highest possible accuracy.

In the frequency response analysis mode, the circuit is first resolved in the DC mode. Then, all non-linear elements are linearized in the neighborhood of the DC operation point. Once the model becomes linear, the state transition matrix is calculated and the frequency analysis performed. The results are presented in the form of the Body plots.

SPICE has huge libraries with thousands of models of electronic devices (diodes, transistors, ICs, SCRs, TRIACs etc.) stored together with their parameters.

SOLIDWORKS

SolidWorks is not exactly a simulation tool, but rather a CAD/CAM program. However, it offers certain 3D features useful in mechanism design and some kind of kinematics simulation.

Following Wikipedia, the main SolidWorks features can be listed as follows. Building a model in SolidWorks usually starts with a 2D sketch (although 3D sketches are available for power users). The sketch consists of geometry such as points, lines, arcs, conics, and splines. Dimensions are added to the sketch to define the size and location of the geometry.

Relations are used to define attributes such as tangency, parallelism, perpendicularity, and concentricity. The parametric nature of SolidWorks means that the dimensions and relations drive the geometry, not the other way around. The dimensions in the sketch can be controlled independently, or by relationships to other parameters inside or outside the sketch.

SolidWorks pioneered the ability of a user to roll back through the history of the part in order to make changes, add additional features, or change to sequence in which operations are performed. Later feature-based solid modeling software also copied this idea.

In an assembly, the analog to sketch relations are mates. Just as sketch relations define conditions such as tangency, parallelism, and concentricity with respect to sketch geometry, assembly mates define equivalent relations with respect to the individual parts or components, allowing the easy construction of assemblies. SolidWorks also includes additional advanced mating features such as gear and cam follower mates, which allow modeled gear assemblies to accurately reproduce the rotational movement of an actual gear train.

Finally, drawings can be created either from parts or assemblies. Views are automatically generated from the solid model, and notes, dimensions and tolerances can then be easily added to the drawing as needed. The drawing module includes most paper sizes and standards

The SolidWorks core product includes tools for 3D modeling, assembly, drawing, sheet-metal, weldments, and freeform surfacing. It can import numerous file types from other 2D and 3D CAD programs. It also has an API for custom programming in Visual Basic and C. Also included is an entry level finite element analysis program called CosmosXpress.

SolidWorks Corporation.
300 Baker Avenue.
Concord, MA 01742.
1-800-693-9000 US and Canada.
+1-978-371-5011 Outside the US and Canada.
info@solidworks.com.

STELLA

It is the one of the most known implementations of the concepts of System Dynamics. A STELLA model is defined in terms of levels and flows. Levels are represented graphically as boxes and flow as directed links (arrows). The levels are integrals of total flows that affect them. The flows can depend on the levels through algebraic functions, depicted as circles. Levels can represent, for example, the capital level of a corporation, the working power or cash. The flows can be cash flow, working power flow, material or machinery flow, etc.

The following figure shows a possible fragment of a STELLA scheme.

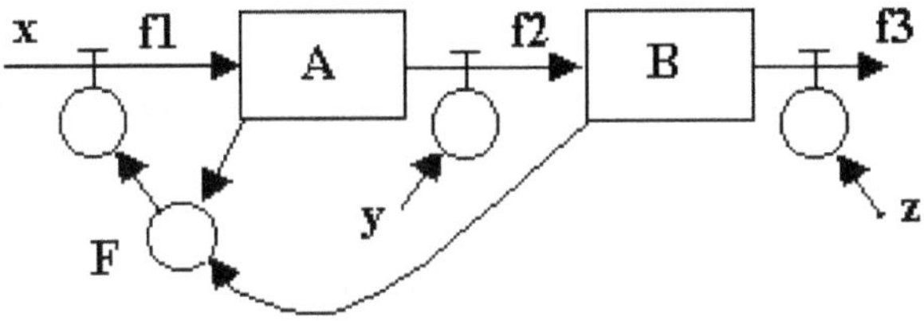

Here, A and B are levels, f1, f2 and f3 are flows and x,y and z are external signals. The flow f1 depends on the levels A and B through the function F.

STELLA, as well as DYNAMO, PowerSim and several other similar tools has been widely used for simulation of dynamic systems in particular in soft systems simulation.

SYSTEM DYNAMICS

System dynamics (SD) is a method for studying the world around us. Unlike other scientists who study the world by breaking it up into smaller and smaller pieces, “system dynamicists” look at things as a whole. The central concept to SD is understanding how all the objects in a system interact with one another.

A system can be anything from a steam engine, to a bank account, to a basketball team. The objects and people in a system interact through “feedback” loops, where a change in one variable affects other variables over time, which in turn affects the original variable, and so on.

System dynamics is a computer-aided approach to policy analysis and design. With origins in servomechanisms engineering and management, the approach uses a perspective based on information feedback and mutual or recursive causality. This helps us understand the dynamics of complex physical, biological, and social systems.

What SD attempts to do is understand the basic structure of a system, and thus, understand the behavior it can produce. Many of these systems and problems which are analyzed can be built as models on a computer. SD takes advantage of the fact that a computer model can be of much greater complexity and carry out more simultaneous calculations than can the mental model of the human mind.

Over the past three decades SD has been applied broadly in such areas as environmental change, economic development, social unrest, urban decay, psychology and physiology.

Jay W. Forrester (http://web.mit.edu/sloan/www/faculty/forrester.html), the creator of System Dynamics, defines it as follows.

Unlike other scientists, who study the world by breaking it up into smaller and smaller pieces, system dynamicists look at things as a whole. The central concept to system dynamics is understanding how all the objects in a system interact with one another. A system can be anything from a steam engine, to a bank account, to a basketball team. The objects and people in a system interact through "feedback" loops, where a change in one variable affects other variables over time, which in turn affects the original variable, and so on.

The seminal book of Jay Forrester Industrial Dynamics (1961) is still a significant statement of philosophy and methodology in the field. Since its publication, the span of applications has grown extensively and now encompasses work in

Corporate planning and policy design
Public management and policy
Biological and medical modeling
Energy and the environment
Theory development in the natural and social sciences
Dynamic decision making
Complex nonlinear dynamics

The System Dynamics Society (SDS) is an international nonprofit organization devoted to encouraging the development and use of systems thinking and system dynamics around the world.

With members in fifty-five countries, the Society provides a forum in which researchers, educators, consultants, practitioners in the corporate and public sectors, interact.

UNIVERSAL MECHANISM

UM was designed to automate the analysis of mechanical objects connected by means of kinematical and force elements.

UM widely applies computer graphics methods to display system's 3D motion in equation process and to analyze the obtained results.

The program is intended for simulation of kinematics and dynamics of planar and spatial mechanical systems. The program is oriented to practical engineers, students and teachers; by other words it is oriented to all people who are involved in problems of dynamics of machines and mechanisms. Mechanical systems are described by means of representing them as systems of rigid bodies connected by various kinematical pairs and force elements. Many dynamical performances of mechanical systems are available during the simulation, such as linear and angular coordinates, velocity and acceleration, active forces and moments, reaction forces etc. UM includes an advanced post-processor: linear analysis, statistics, optimization, exports of results. Discount for students and scientists.

Postal address:

Laboratory of Computational Mechanics

Bryansk State Technical University

bulv. 50-let Oktyabrya, 7, Bryansk, 241035, Russia

Phone, fax: +7 4832 568637

VISSIM

VisSim is a Windows-based program for the modeling and simulation of complex nonlinear dynamic systems. VisSim combines an intuitive drag and drop block diagram interface with a powerful simulation engine. It is the core engine for the VisSim/Comm and VisSim/Embedded Controls Developer products. VisSim/Comm is a software tool for the modelling and simulation of end-to-end, physical layer communication systems.

VisSim/Embedded Controls Developer™ lets you simulate and generate C-code for embedded systems. Save months of design and debug time for fixed-point and floating point targets. Implement hardware features such as SCI, SPI, PWM, CAN, QEP, analogue I/O, and digital I/O at the click of a mouse.

"Due to its power, flexibility, ease-of-use, and low cost, VisSim has been Carrier's choice for system modelling, simulation, data acquisition, and rapid prototyping for over ten years."

VisSim is a winner of EDN's Hot 100 top technologies

Contact:

Adept Scientific brings you Vissim/Embedded Controls Developer for DSPs in partnership with Kane Computing Ltd - a specialist provider of hardware and software tools for DSP development.

Call +44 (0)1606 351006 to make an enquiry about Vissim/ECD or email sales@kanecomputing.com

Chapter 4

Discrete Event Modeling & Simulation

General concepts

Imagine a small barbershop with one client queue and one barber.

Let the aim of our simulation be to observe how the client queue changes during a workday. What really influence the queue length are the client arrival rate and the average service time. In order to satisfy our simulation aim we do not need to simulate how a client moves inside the shop or how much he/she weighs. What we must simulate are *events* like arrival, seizing the server (start service) and releasing the server (be served, go out). These events can be supposed to happen in a discrete time instants. In other words, we will not simulate the process of opening the door and passing from the door to the waiting line. We suppose that each one of these events occurs instantly. So, the events occur in certain time instants, and nothing happens between consecutive events. This means that the model time can jump from one event to another. The model time is a real variable, but takes a discrete, maybe random, values. This is what happens in discrete event simulation: only the events are simulated, and the time does not advance continuously, but rather in finite intervals. In this way, we achieve a good speedup of the simulation.

The problem is, however, how to manage the event queue (not the client queue of our example) inside the simulation system. The model time must jump to the next event, so we must every time select the nearest event or to maintain the *event queue* sorted by the execution time. Anyway, this is always the problem of sorting. A simple linear search or sorting where we scan the whole set of events can work with few possible events, but becomes very slow when the number of events grows. As it is a sorting problem, it will not be discussed here in detail. Note only that a discrete event simulation package is so good as good is its event queue management.

The first discrete simulation languages like CSL had simple, but already good implementations of the event queue management. Then, different strategies of the event scheduling and process interaction appeared. See the section “Strategies of Discrete Event Simulation.”

Strategies of Discrete Event Simulation

There are three basic strategies in discrete simulation: Activity scanning (AS), Event scheduling (ES), and Process interaction (PI). In this section, we treat *activity* and *event* as synonyms. More advanced strategies are being developed and can be found in publications on the DEVS (Discrete Event Specification Formalism).

Activity Scanning (AS) was the first discrete simulation strategy, developed in the 1950s. One of the first implementations was the language CSL - Control and Simulation Language. According to this strategy, the model time is set equal to the time instant of the nearest event. Then, all model activities (events) are scanned and those that can be executed, are, the others remain inactive. Next, the time jumps to the next possible event, and the whole process is repeated. This clock loop stops if no possible events remain in the model. An event, while being executed, can schedule itself or other events, to be executed in the future. So the event sequence can be long and complicated, even if the source program is relatively short.

The *Event Scheduling* (ES) strategy is somewhat more effective. In the computer memory the *event queue* is created. Every component or *event message* of this queue stores the time the event will be executed, and the event identifier. So, the only problem is to maintain the event queue sorted according to execution time. If we do this, then we simply take the first event and execute it, without scanning all possible events. This event queue management is transparent (invisible for the user) and works automatically. The user can schedule events, but cannot redefine the model time or manipulate directly the event queue. The most effective event management algorithms are those that use binary tree techniques to sort the event queue.

The *Process Interaction* (PI) strategy is more advanced. The model is defined in terms of processes that can run concurrently. The rules of interactions between processes are defined, while the specification of a process includes the necessary event scheduling. PI can be implemented in any object-oriented programming language, and became the main feature of Simula, Modsim, BLUESSS and other languages.

The *Three phase strategy* in discrete simulation is a combination of these three strategies. The three phases are as follows.

1. Model time jumps to the next event.
2. The event(s) scheduled to be executed at this time instant are executed.
3. All state- and conditional events are revised. Those that can be executed, are.

See "Event queue" and "Distributed simulation."

Consult:

O'Keefe R.M., The three-phase approach: A comment on strategy-related characteristics of discrete event languages and models, SIMULATION, 47(5), November 1986, pp. 208-210.

Lin J.T., Lee Chia-Chu, A three-phase discrete event simulation with EPNSim graphs, SIMULATION, 60(6), June 1993, pp. 382-392.

See also "DEVS," "Distributed simulation"

The event queue

Let us recall how the clock mechanism of one of the first simulation languages Control and Simulation Language, CSL, 1950s) has been working. A series of time variables (TVs) were defined, each one related to a model event. The TVs were "placed" on the time axis. The model time was jumping to the nearest (in time) TV. Then, this time interval was subtracted from all the TVs. So, there was always one or more TVs with value equal to zero. This made it possible to use a simple logical condition (is the TV equal to zero?) in the event execution. Each event could modify all the TVs and create new ones.

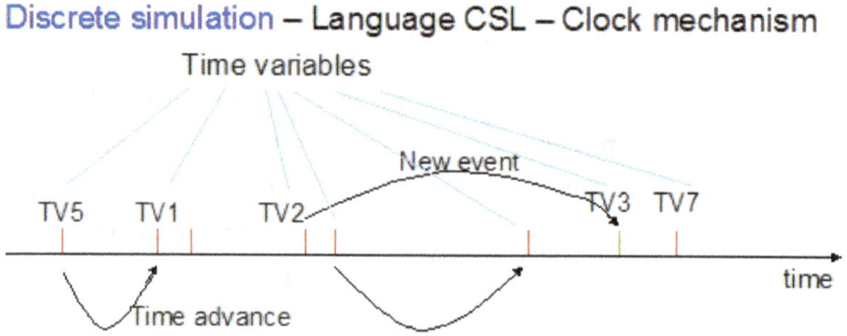

This simple mechanism controlled the model time and the event execution.

Observe that in this algorithm, the TVs form a queue on the time axis, where the first event to execute is that which has the smallest value of the corresponding TV. So, the sorting problem arises: the system must maintain the queue ordered due to the TVs ("time stamps"). Otherwise, it would have to look for the next event each time before an event execution. Anyway, we have the sorting problem.

In other, discrete-event and object-oriented simulation languages or packages, the CSL TVs are replaced by event messages. An event message is a data structure with its time-stamp and the data about the event to execute (event ID, a pointer to a method, etc.). The figure below illustrates this mechanism.

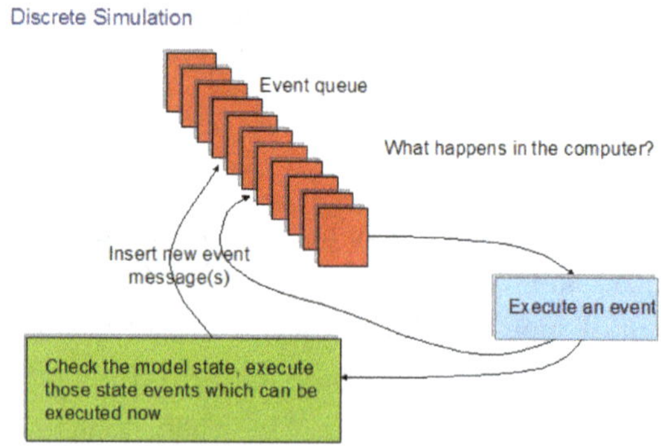

The event queue management is the most important feature of any discrete event simulation system.

If the event queue is stored as a simple linear array of event messages, the sorting problem needs N (N-1)/2 comparisons in average. This may take considerable computer time, taking into account that, even for simple models, the queue may contain thousands of event messages. There are some algorithms that can accelerate this process. One of them is the Binary Tree Search (BTS) method.

A binary tree is made of nodes, where each node contains a "left" pointer, a "right" pointer, and a data element. The "root" pointer points to the topmost node in the tree. A "binary search tree" (BST) or "ordered binary tree" is a type of binary tree where the nodes are arranged in order: for each node, all elements in its left sub-tree are less-or-equal to the node (<=), and all the elements in its right sub-tree are greater than the node (>). See the example below:

Sequence of numbers: 3, 8, 1, 22, 17, 2, 0, 45, 7

Binary tree (BTS)

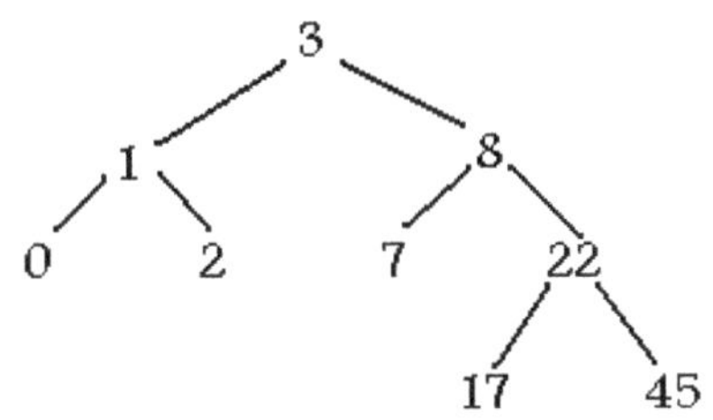

To construct the tree simply put the consecutive numbers in places no occupied yet. If the number is less or equal to the number at the previous node, put it at the left-hand sub-node, otherwise put it at the right. Note that to do it we need few comparisons. For example, to put the number "2" at its place, we do not need to compare it with 8, 7 22 17 or 45.

The search for the minimal number is also very quick. Starting with the root of the tree, go to the left until there is no left-hand sub-node.

Most of contemporary simulation systems use this method to maintain the internal event queue.

Discrete Event Simulation Formalism (DEVS)

The Discrete Event Specification (DEVS) formalism is used to describe models in discrete event simulation. In the DEVS formalism, a model M is defined as follows.

$$M = < X, S, Y, \sigma_{int}, \sigma_{ext}, \lambda, \tau > \qquad (1)$$
$$\sigma_{int} : S \rightarrow S$$

where X is the input space, S is the system state space, Y is the output space, s_{int} is the internal state transition function, s_{ext} is the external transition function and Q is the "total state."

$$\sigma_{ext} : Q \times S \rightarrow S$$
$$Q = \{(s,e) \mid s \in S, 0 \leq e \leq ta(s)\}$$

Here, e is the elapsed time since last state transition. The term $ta(s)$ is the time of an internal state transition when no external event occurs.

$$\lambda : Q \rightarrow Y$$

is the output function, and τ is the time-advance function. The DEVS model (1) is also called basic model. To treat complex models with variable structure, the Dynamic Structure Discrete Event System Specification (DSDEVS) is used. This formalism includes DSDEVN dynamic structure network that is the pair *<h, Mh>*, where *h* is the network executive name, and *Mh* is the model of *h*. It was pointed out that the DSDEVS formalism is closed under coupling. This allows to use the formalism while building more complex models using re-usable sub-models.

Consult

Chow A.C., Zeigler, B, 1994, Parallel DEVS: A Parallel, Hierarchical, Modular Modeling Formalism, Proceedings of the 1994 Winter Simulation Conference

Zeigler B.P., Hierarchical, modular discrete-event modelling in an object-oriented environment, SIMULATION 49(5), pp.219-230

Srivastava A., Rammohan K.R., Object-oriented Simulation of a SIMD Computer Using OMT and DEVS Methodology, Proceedings of the Object Oriented Simulation Conference (OOS'94)

Distributed Simulation

While there are many ways simulation speed can be improved, clearly the most important is to move from sequential to parallel execution. This means that the modeling and simulation task is distributed between multiple processors at the same mainframe or in separate computers running in a network. The fundamental issue is the extent to which simulations should be synchronized in a conservative manner. In distributed simulation each processor runs with its own model time clock. Several distributed simulation techniques have been developed, like Chandy-Misra algorithm (Chandy K.M., Holmes V. and Misra J., Distributed simulation of networks, Computer Networks vol.3, no.1, February 1979, pp.105-113), and the Time Warp algorithm (Jefferson D. and Sowizral H. Fast concurrent simulation using the Time Warp mechanism, Distributed Simulation 1985, The 1985 Society of Computer Simulation Multiconference, San Diego, California). The former is pessimistic or conservative, advancing the processor simulation clocks only when conditions permit. In contrast, Time Warp assumes the simulation clocks can be advanced until conflicting information appears; the clocks are then rolled back to a consistent state.

Such conflict situation arises when one of the local clocks (say that of processor A) advances more quickly than some other (processor B). If the object simulated on processor B sends a message to that of processor A, the message arrives in the object past. However, every received message can change the object behavior, so the object on A must return to the (past) moment of the message and repeat its, perhaps different, trajectory. The situation complicates if the object A have issued messages to other objects after the model time instant of the conflict. All these messages must be cancelled and the receiving object must also roll back their clocks. This may result in a chain of rollbacks, and make the simulation even slower than in the pessimistic mode.

Distributed simulation has no application on single machines and PCs. It is being implemented rather on supercomputers, computer networks and machines with multiple processors. Applications belong mostly to aircraft simulation, communication networks, defense strategy, VLSI chips and similar great-scale models

Random numbers

In many simulation tasks, like discrete event simulation or stochastic models, appear random variables. These are variables that can take random values, and have well defined probabilistic properties. Main properties include the probability distribution, expected value, variance, and confidence intervals among others. Sometimes, we have to face models that include uncertain variables. A common way to treat such model uncertainty is to use stochastic models and random variables. However, note that an uncertain variable not always can be modeled as random one. An uncertain value may be just uncertain, and may have no probabilistic properties. This may occur, for example, when the probabilistic properties are unknown, or when the variable is generated in the environment, like an intentional false information in models with human factor.

The random variables and probability distributions are frequently included in simulation books and manuals, though this is rather the topic of the theory of probabilities and statistics.

Probability cumulative and density functions

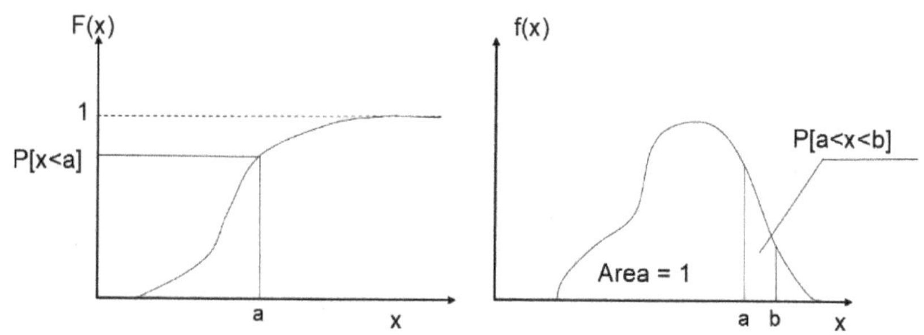

Figure 1. Probability cumulative and density functions (continuous distribution).

The *probability cumulative function* is defined as a non-decreasing function $F(x)$, such that $F(a)=P[x<a]$ (probability that x is less than a). Figure one shows an example of a continuous cumulative and density functions. In figure two, we can see an example of a *discrete distribution*. Note that the density function is defined using the delta pulse functions. The coefficient that multiplies a consecutive pulse at $x=a$ is the probability that $x=a$.

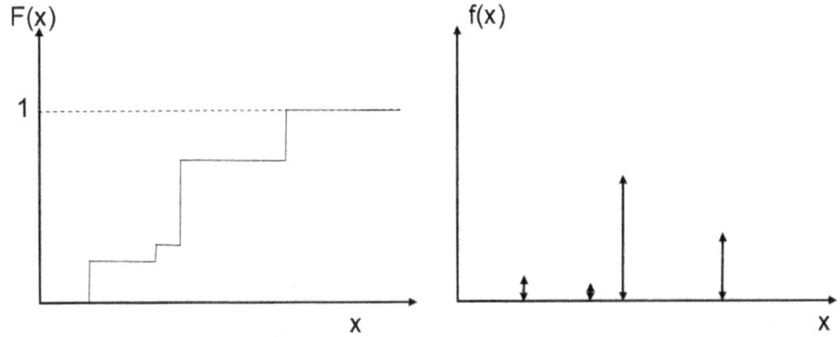

Discrete distribution: Probability cumulative and density functions.

Consult: William Feller, "An Introduction to Probability Theory and Its Applications," Vol. 1, 3rd Edition, 1968, Wiley.

Uniform distribution

The uniform or rectangular distribution describes a random variable uniformly distributed within a non-empty interval.

Normal distribution

$$f(x) = \frac{1}{\sigma\sqrt{2\pi}} \exp\left(\frac{-(x-\mu)^2}{2\sigma^2}\right)$$

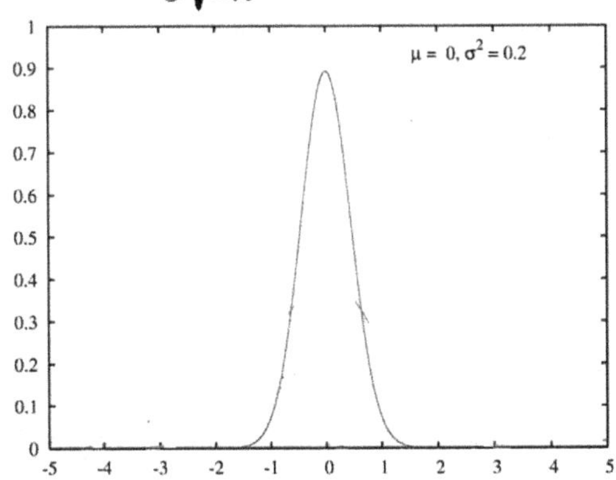

Example of normal distribution: density function.

Example: Prey-Predator discrete model with herd instinct

General Remarks

Recall that in the discrete object-based modeling, we create objects that behave according to the user-defined rules, executing their events in discrete moments of the model time. The agent-based models (ABMs) manage objects called agents, equipped with certain "intelligence." They can take decisions, optimize their actions and interact with each other. The agents may be of different types. Although the rules of behavior are shared by a group of agents of the same type, the behavior is not identical for all of them. This modeling method has many applications, mainly in ecology, biology and social sciences. A key notion is that simple behavioral rules (micro model) generate complex (macro) behavior. An important central tenet is that the whole is greater than the sum of the parts.

Observe that the results presented here are quite different from the results provided by a simple Lotka-Volterra prey-predator model.

Simulation Tool

The BLUESSS (Blues Simulation System) package was used to simulate the prey-predator model. The main of the package are as follows.

- Object-oriented simulation
- Continuous/discrete models
- Clock mechanism
- Inheritance
- Permits the use of all C++ features
- Easy to use, clear process/event structure

The BLUESSS package is described in section "General Purpose Software Tools."

The model

Below, there is a short description of the BLUESSS implementation of the model. The technical details and the corresponding code are not included.

The main BLUESSS process of the model is entity. One of the attributes of the entity is the type, equal to zero for prey and equal to one for the predator. Inside the entity declarations there are several declarations of events. The possible events are as follows.

* Move

* Seek a food (if prey)

* Look for a prey (if predator)

* Eat (the prey eats the limited and renewable food, the predator eats the prey)
* Escape (the prey type)
* Follow the herd (gregarious) instinct
* Reproduce
* Evolve
* Die (natural death or being devoured)
* Die, as a consequence of epidemics or other external events

There are two more processes: food and display.

The food process has, at the run time, only one instance. The region where the entities move is a rectangle. It is divided into 400 rectangle spots, each of them having a uniform distribution of food. When a prey consumes food, then the amount of food in the corresponding spot decreases, and the prey energy increases. The longer time it eats, the more energy accumulates. The amount of food changes between 0 (no food) and 1 (max food). The food is renewable and the amount of food slowly increases in time. This is controlled by an event of the food process. If the prey entity does not eat for some long time interval, it dies. This does not occur if the food mechanism is disabled.

The evolution consists of small changes in the entity attributes in the process of reproduction, so that the next generations may change their behavior. This mechanism, as well as the specification of entity attributes, is described further on.

The direction of entity movement v is the normalized sum of several factors: is calculated as $v = Gg + Rr + Ee + Ff$, where g is the gregarious movement direction, r is the random walk, e is the chase/escape direction and f is the direction for food seeking. G, R, E and F are corresponding coefficients.

The display process repeatedly shows the model state, i.e. the positions of all entities, the directions of movement, the state of food resource. This produces an animated image of the whole model. There is another auxiliary process named immigration that slowly generates new prey and predator objects. This process was introduced to avoid the situation when the prey or predator population reaches zero and no further reproduction is possible.

The model can run in several modes, according to the possible events. The modes are:

1. Simple mode (no food mechanism, no gregarious instinct, movement only according to the random walk, no evolution, no epidemics).
2. Gregarious effect on/off.
3. Food on/off.
4. Fear on/off.
5. Movement direction on/off. This means the predator does not follow the prey, and the prey does not detect the predator and escapes. The entities move by the random walk.
6. Evolution on/off.
7. Epidemics on/off.

The program permits to define the mode as simple, or as any combination of the modes 2-6. This means that, even without changing the parameters of the entities, we can carry out great number of experiments. Here, only some more interesting results are described.

Simulation experiments

In our model, the declaration of process "entity" includes several parameters that are "attached" to the objects. Each instant of a new object has its own set of attributes. The values of the attributes are defined at the moment of the object creation, by the reproduction or other event. The attributes include:

* object position (x,y) inside the simulated area
* object type (prey or predator)
* movement directions v, g, r, e and f (explained below)
* energy
* overall activity time step
* inheritance factor
* array of auxiliary parameters p1, p2, p3....

Here, due to limited room, we only give a general description of entity actions.

Actual movement direction is given by the (vector) attribute v. This direction is the normalized weighted sum of the following directions:

r - random walk direction
g - direction of herd instinct movement
e - escape direction for prey, chase direction for predator
f - food seeking direction (prey)
v - actual direction of movement. $v = Gg + Rr + Ee + Ff$, where G, R, E and F are constant coefficients

The parameters pi define the following.

* the weight for herd instinct (Gregarious) direction
* the weight for random walk
* actual fear factor and fear grow factor
* average life time (for natural death)
* time step for food seeking (prey)
* the time interval for food eating (prey stops to eat)
* food seeking velocity

The above attributes control the movement and other actions of the entity. The main actions are as follows.

Random walk. The entity moves in random direction.

Herd (Gregarious) movement. The entity calculates the direction as a normalized weighted sum of the directions of its neighbors. The weight is greater for nearby neighbors.

Escape/chase direction. The predator looks for the nearest prey and follows it. The prey detects the nearest predator and intents to escape.

Fear. The fear factor of the prey (one of the parameters p) grows when a nearby predator is detected. This increases the escape velocity and decreases the time interval for eating food.

Energy. Each entity has the energy, initialized with value 1. While moving, the energy decreases. If it reaches zero, the entity dies. However, when a prey eats the food, its energy grows, so it can recuperate its entire energy (level one).

Life time, death. When being created, the entity is provided the value of its average time interval for the natural death (LT). The lifetime is calculated as a random variable with expected value LT and negative-exponential distribution. However, the entity may die before, for the energy lost of being devoured.

Food. As explained in the previous section, the food level in the spot where a prey is eating decreases. The food is renewable, and the speed of food increase is controlled by the food process.

Reproduction and evolution (prey). The rate of reproduction for the prey depends on its energy. When the energy decreases, the reproduction rate decreases also. If the energy level is less than 0.7 the prey cannot reproduce. The reproduction consists in creating a new prey object. It appears near its parent object and inherits all the attributes from the parent. If evolution is on, then the inherited attributes are changed a little bit, depending on the inheritance factor attribute. This way, next generations of prey may change their behavior.

Reproduction (predator). The predator can reproduce only if it devours a prey. So, if the prey population grows, the predator population grows also, with some delay. If there are little or no prey objects, predators die with their natural death.

Epidemics. This represents the other cause of entity death. A prey object may be affected by certain disease that accelerates its death. If a predator devours an ill entity, it also become infected and dies.

Results: Random Walk

The models simulated below are not related to any real ecological system, and provide only some qualitative and behavioral properties that a real system may reveal. Consequently, the time unit is undefined, may be interpreted, for example, as months. In all experiments there is an automatic lower limit of population size, set to two entities. So, no population can completely disappear.

In this experiment, the simulation mode is set to random walk only. The prey, as well as the predator move according to the random walk. When a predator position is near to a prey (less than 0.05 of the size of the whole region), then the prey is devoured and the predator can reproduce.

For all prey objects the energy does not decrease and they can reproduce with given reproduction rate. It might appear that in such case (random prey-predator encounters) the simulation results should be similar as those of basic L-V model (1). However, this is not the case. Fig. 1 shows the results of the simulation.

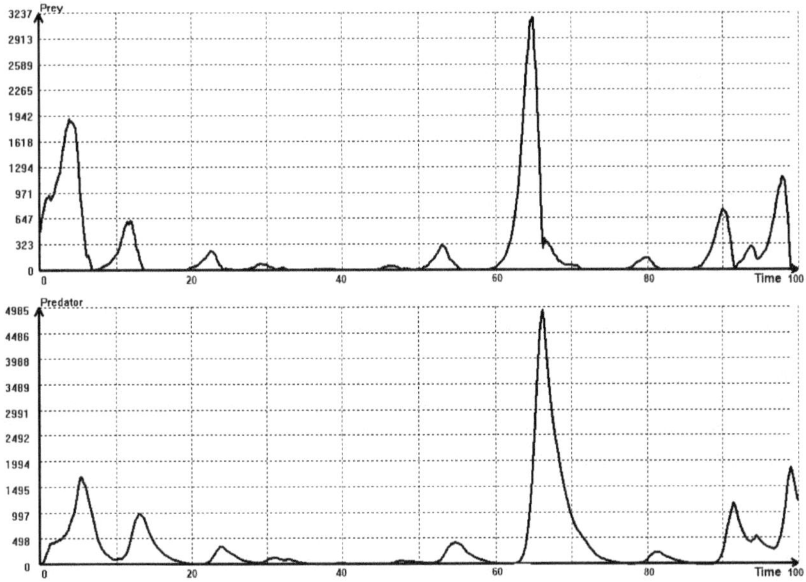

Figure 1. Random walk only.
The population changes for the prey and predator.

It can be seen that the behavior of the two species is very irregular. Though we could look for an approximate period of population growth, the local maximal values are very different. For this irregular values, any statistics over the populations are little informative. This discrepancy between the L-V model and ABM simulation can be explained by the spatial distribution of the entities. The entities move randomly, but the reproduction process creates new entities in the neighborhood of parent object. As a result, we observe formation of clusters. If a prey cluster appears near some predators, it is devoured. However, when the cluster forms in some distance of the predators, the cluster starts to grow exponentially, until the predator random movement makes it possible to devour the preys.

Chase and Escape Direction on

Now, the movement direction is a combination of chase direction (predator) and escape direction (prey). Figure 2 shows the situation over the simulated region, for time equal to 77. The clusters and the escape/chase direction can be seen. In the following simulation, if not stated differently, the initial population of prey is equal to 500 and the initial number of predator is 50.

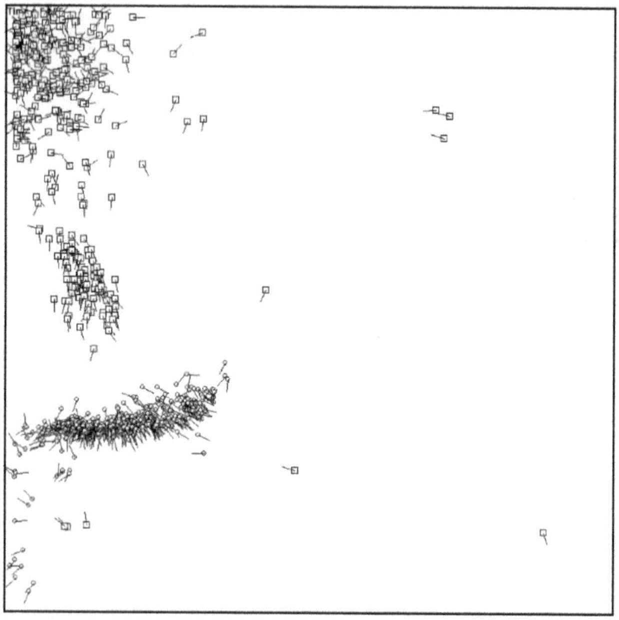

Figure 2. Screenshot of model animation, chase/escape on. Rectangle objects are predators, circular are preys. The small line sections indicate movement direction.

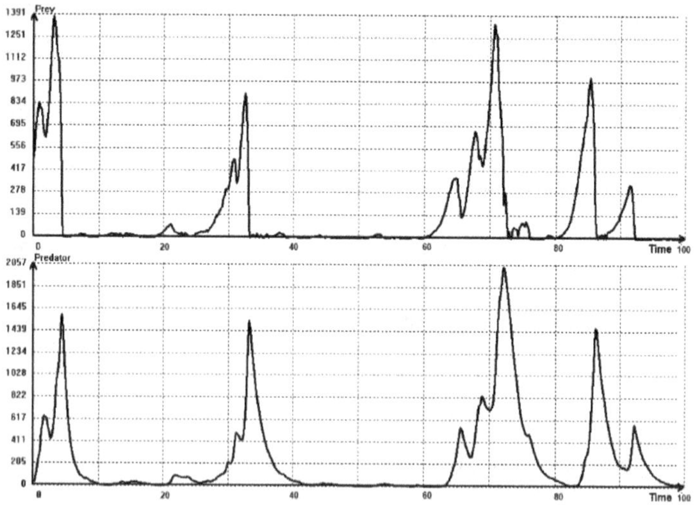

Figure 3. Prey and predator population changes, chase/escape direction on.

Figure 3 depicts the changes of the two populations. The changes are still highly irregular, with several big maxima. Compared to the plot of fig.1, perhaps the period of the cycles (where they are seen) is smaller in this case. Looking at the animations for this case it can be observed that the model behavior is highly irregular and unpredictable. If the prey can form cluster in some area with few predators, its population may grow exponentially. In general, the simulations in this, as well in some other cases, are little repetitive. This means that the statistics that can be taken over a series of consecutive simulations with the same parameters are little informative. In particular, the average value of the populations (as function of time) does not provide any relevant information. In section 4.9 below you can find some examples of the variance analysis taken over a set of trajectories. In many cases the variance is very high. Recall that using the classic continuous models we get the same results in repetitive simulations with the same parameters. This is one of the relevant differences between agent-based and continuous system dynamics modeling.

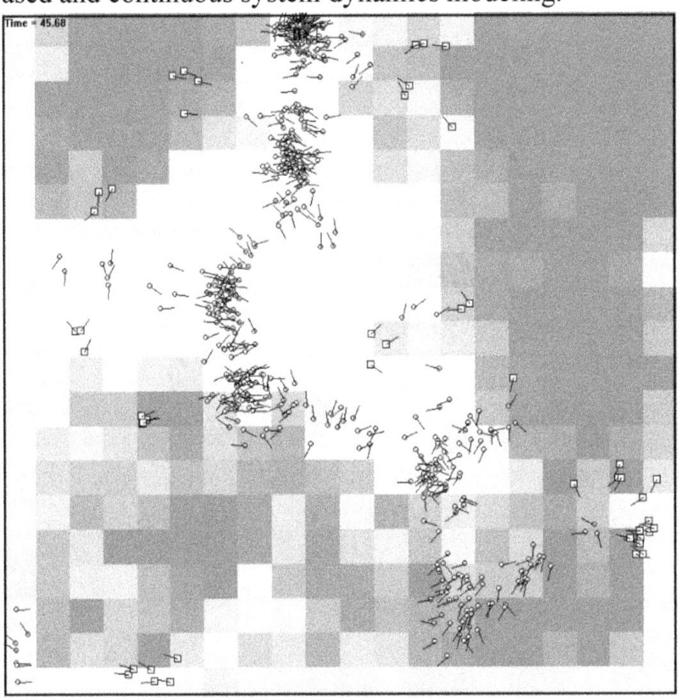

Figure 4. Chase/escape on, food on.

Food, chase, escape on

In fig.4 we can see the simulated area with food enabled. The gray spot has 100% of food, and the white spot has no food. Prey entities are looking for nearest spot with food, move there and stop a while to eat. The food is renewable. If there is no prey at the spot, the food level in the spot slowly increases,

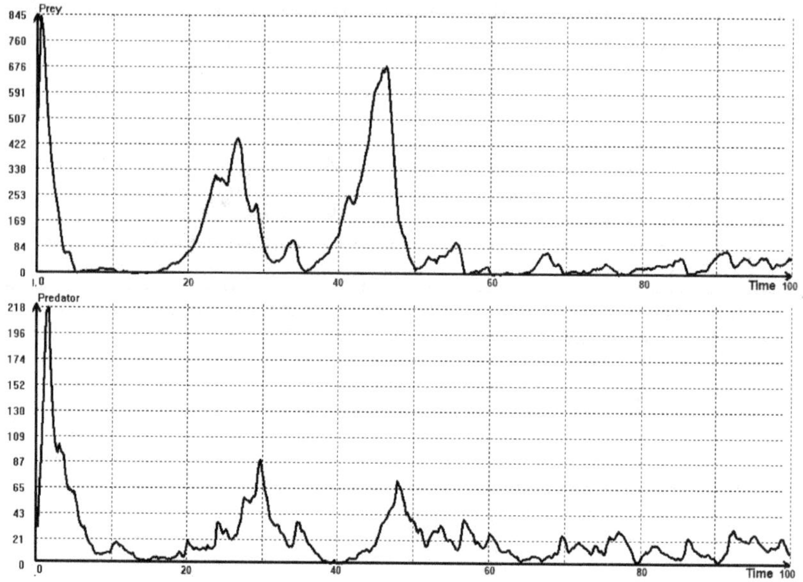

Figure 5. Population changes. Chase/escape on, food on

The changes of the two populations are shown on fig. 5. Note that with limited food resource the population changes are more regular. The population of prey cannot grow too much, because of lack of food at the spots where they actually are. Compare to fig.3 (food off), where the prey population reaches 1247, while with limited food (fig.5) the maximal prey population is equal to 717 just after simulation starts, but then it is no greater than 700 entities for the rest of the period.

Gregarious Instinct

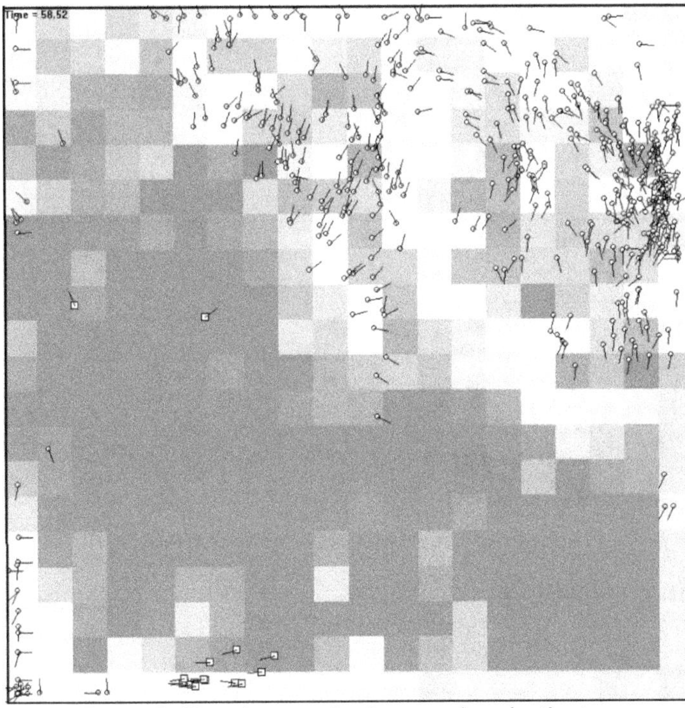

Figure 6. Chase/escape, food, gregarious instinct on.

Now, we add the gregarious instinct to the behavior of the entities. Looking at the animations, it can be seen that both pray and predator form more clusters with similar movement direction. Note that the clusters have also been formed without gregarious effect, according to the chase/escape direction. However, it seems that the gregarious effect makes the escape and hunting processes quicker, so that any cycles in the population size can hardly be seen. Also, the total population in this simulation mode is rather low after the initial "warm up" interval. This is according to the fact that the entities hunt and escape more efficiently. Anyway, looking at the plots of fig. 5 and 7, it can be seen that the population changes are completely different from that of the continuous L

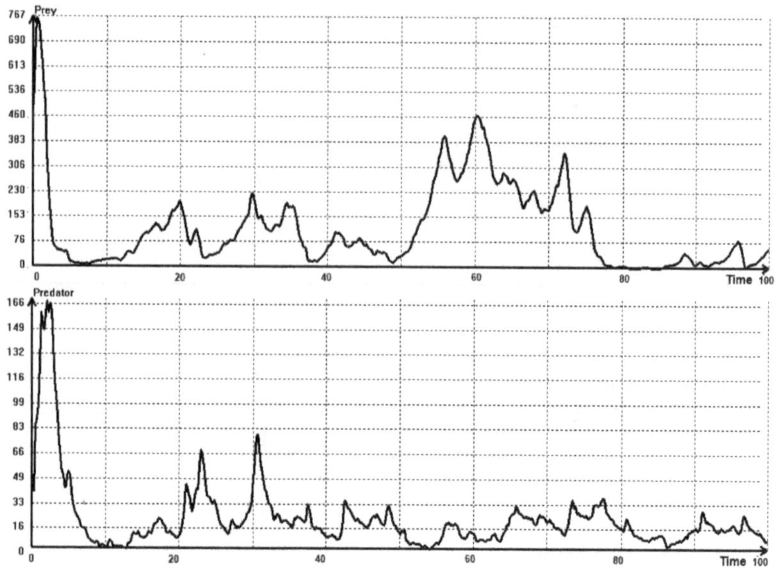

Figure 7. Time plot: Chase/escape, food, gregarious instinct on.

Fear, Food and Energy

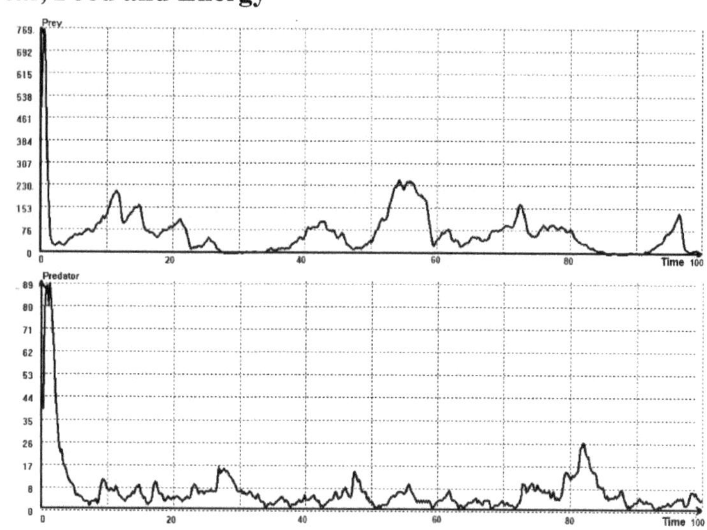

Figure 8. Population changes with fear on.

In this model the fear is introduced by simple modifications of the prey escape velocity and eating time. If a prey detects a nearby predator, its fear attribute increases. If there are no predators in the neighborhood and fear attribute is greater than one, then the attribute decreases. The escape velocity is multiplied by the fear attribute. The eating time of the prey is divided by the attribute, because the entity prefers rather to escape than eat. The increased escape velocity makes it more difficult for the predator to devour the prey. On the other hand, the prey does not recuperate its energy and may slow down or die. Figure 8 shows the corresponding plots of population changes.

In this case the fear has two opposite effects: greater escape velocity, less food eaten. The effect is not very clearly seen from the plots. However, observe that the predator population is lower with fear on, perhaps because the prey escapes quickly. The low population level is mainly the result of limited food. To see the influence of this resource let us suppose that the prey recuperates three times more energy while eating the food. This augments the prey to lifetime and its escape velocity. Figure 9 depicts the corresponding population changes. Both the prey and predator population size is greater in this case. However, the irregular shape of the plots remains.

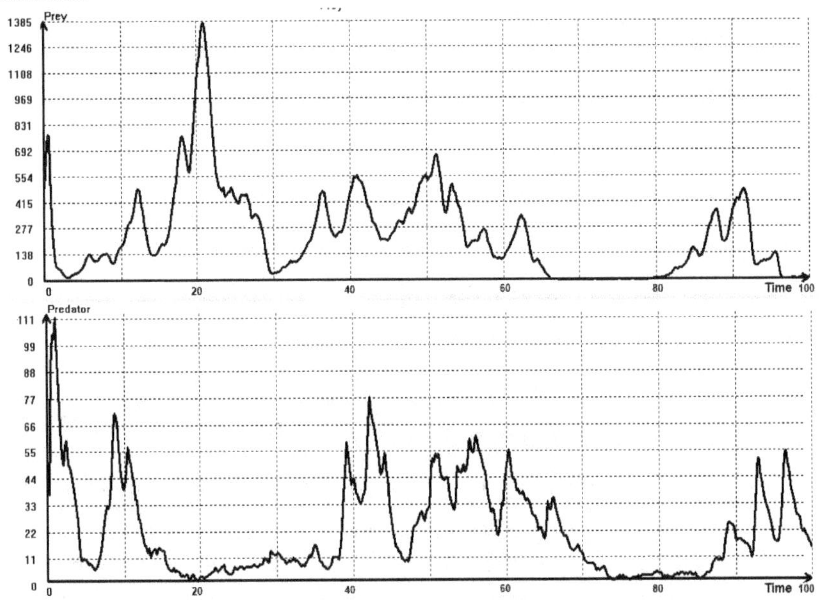

Figure 9. More prey energy.

Epidemics

This model feature may be interpreted as anything that may influence the population. It may be a disease, a natural disaster or human action.

Here, we rather simulate a disease because the entities can be infected by near contact and the predator can be infected by devouring an infected prey. The disease appears randomly one or more times during the simulated period.

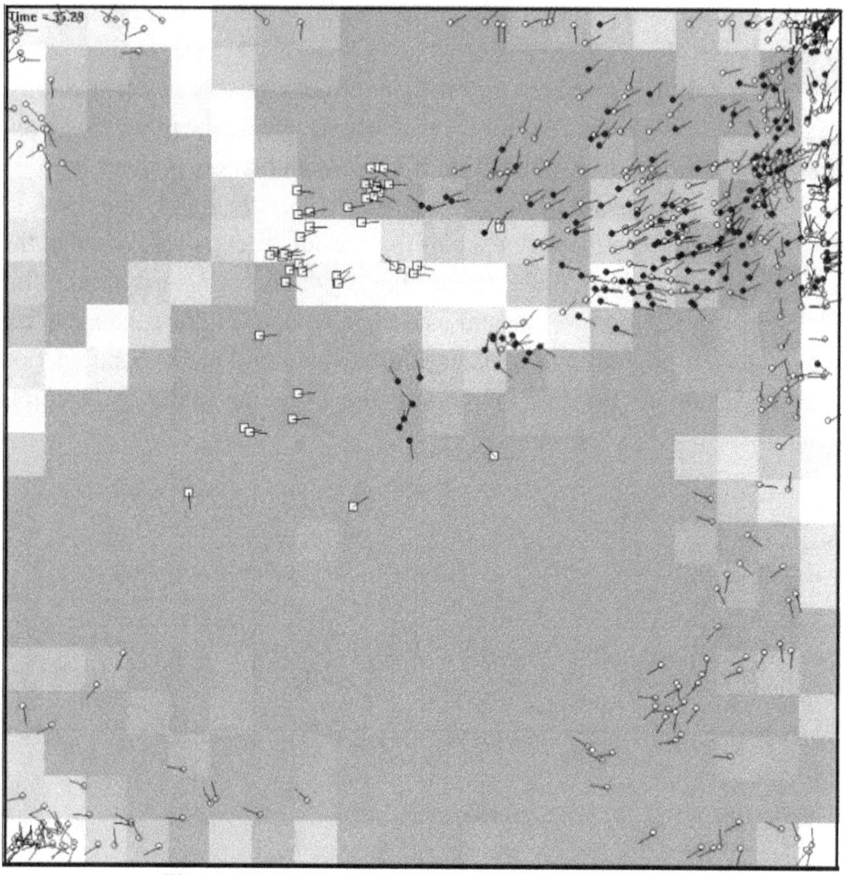

Figure 10. Epidemics. Black entities are infected.

The population changes in this case are even more chaotic. The infected entities can be seen in figure 10 (prey with black circles). These entities die quickly after being infected. The effect can be seen in figure 11. Observe that the epidemics may affect the whole population (the last event) or only a part of it. This depends again on the actual spatial distribution of the individuals.

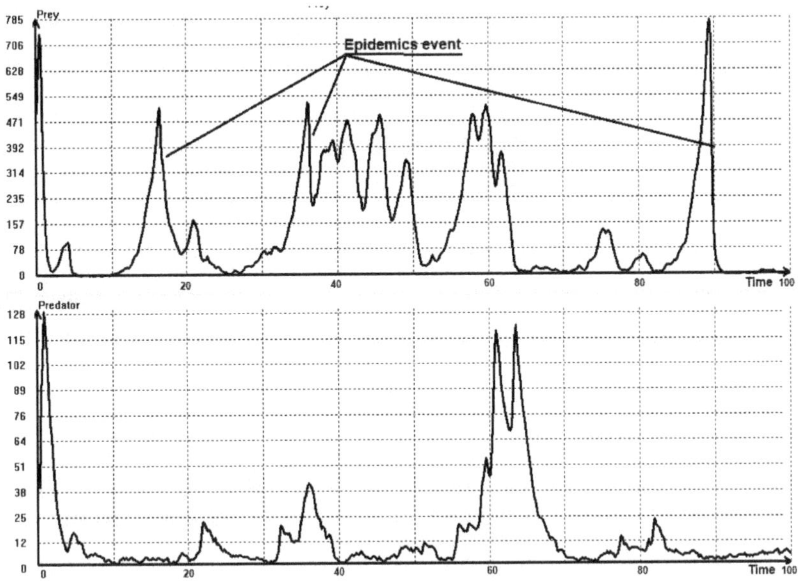

Figure 11. Population changes with epidemics.

Evolution

With evolution enabled, some entity attributes are slightly changed during the reproduction event. The new entity inherits the modified attributes and passes them, also modified, in the next reproduction event. With longer simulation time (1000 time units instead of 100 as before), the attributes slowly change their average value. Note that in the simulation program there is no explicit instruction that could force the attributes to increase or to decrease their values.

The evolution is enabled for prey only. The attributes of interest are gregarious factor and the food eating time of the prey. Recall that the direction of entity movement is calculated as $v = Gg + Rr + Ee + Ff$, where g is the gregarious movement direction, r is the random walk, e is the chase/escape direction and f is the direction for food seeking. In this experiment, the initial values of the coefficients are G=0.2, R=0.1, E=0.3 and F=0.1. The initial value of the food eating time is 0.18 time units.

From the model events it is not clear if the gregarious effect helps the prey to escape or not. The influence of eating time is also uncertain. On the one hand the prey gains energy while eating food. On the other hand, the prey must stop to eat and may be easily devoured by the predator.

During reproduction, both G and eating time are changed randomly within the interval plus minus 0.015.

In fig. 12 we can see the result of the prey evolution over 1000 time units. This corresponds to, approximately, 600 "generations" of prey, where the average prey lifetime is equal to 1.7. The plots show the average values of the items, taken over the actual prey population at each time instant. We can see that the tendency for the gregarious coefficient is positive, changing from 0.2 to approximately 0.5 with final value of 0.4. The prey eating time also grows, from 0.18 to nearly 3.5 time units.

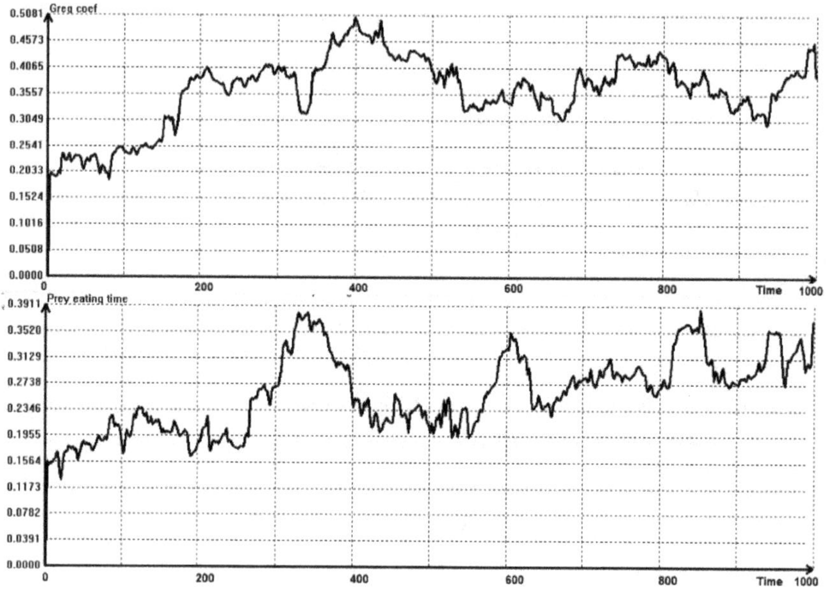

Figure 12. Prey evolution: changes of gregarious coefficient and eating time.

Variance Analysis

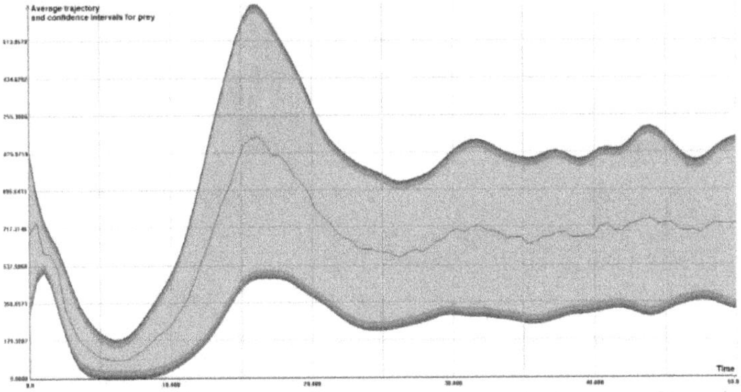

Figure 13. Average trajectory and confidence intervals for prey. Chase/escape, food, gregarious instinct enabled. Vertical axis shows population size.

Frequently, statistics like average value of variance are calculated and used to compare options or make decisions. However, if model variables have big variance and range of extreme values, the usefulness of such statistics questionable. In particular, the average trajectories for models with great variance can be calculated, but they provide little useful information. Fortunately, the BLUESSS system provides tools for such type of analysis. Fig. 13 shows the confidence intervals for the trajectories of the model used in section "food, gregarious, chase/escape on." The gray region indicates where the prey population belongs with probability equal to 0.9. The line inside the region is the average trajectory. The image was obtained from 100 repetitions of the simulation run. It can be seen that the fluctuations with confidence level 0.9 are approximately equal to 50% of the average trajectory. This confirms the fact that the average provides little relevant information.

Competition

In fig.14 we can see the changes of the two populations competing for a common resource, obtained from the agent-based model. Here, both species have the same parameters. The food is renewable. The food seeking direction and the gregarious effect are enabled. It can be seen that the simulation results are completely different from those of the continuous model. In general, there is no "winner" of this food-seeking game.

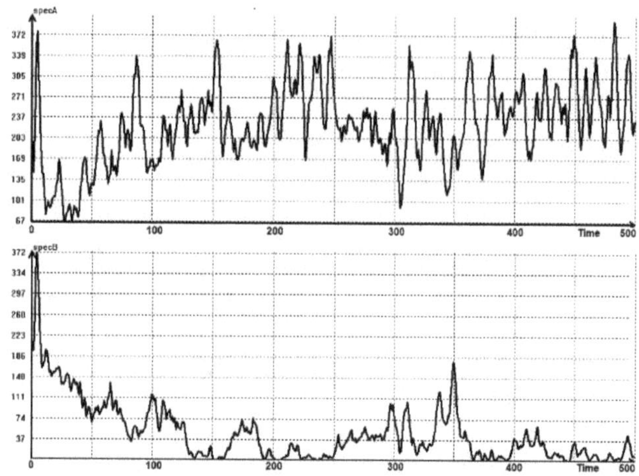

Figure 14. Agent-based simulation of competing species. Gragarious instinct and evolution enabled.

The plots show the evolution of the ratio G/R, calculated as the average over corresponding populations, every time-step. It can be seen that the species A evolved to lower values of this ratio, this means less gregarious and more random walk, while the species B did not. Note that there is no explicit instruction in the model code that could force such evolution. The conclusion is that, in this case, the herd instinct does not help to survive.

Here, only some of possible experiments are discussed. The agent-based models (ABM) are perhaps more realistic than the continuous Lotka-Volterra differential equation (ODE) models. The ABM models permit us simulate the spatial distribution and movements of the entities, and to take into account many behavioral patterns. The general conclusion is that the agent-based simulation provides results quite different from the ODE models. As for the classic L-V model it has been pointed out that, while treated with the differential inclusions, the results with uncertain parameters show a high uncertainty, even with final time equal to one oscillation period. The ABM models also reveal the high-variance trajectory fluctuations. This might be reduced by simulating population with greater number of individuals. However, in this case the program slows down considerably. The initial populations set equal to 500 and 50 for prey and predator, respectively, make the computer simulation time acceptable.

ABM model permits limited food resource, herd instinct, random movement, competition, fear and evolution. Note that the behavior of the whole simulated population is not a "sum" of the individual behavior patterns. For example, the direction of the parameter's evolution has not been explicitly coded in the events of the individuals. However, in some experiments, we obtain clear evolution tendencies.

Waiting lines

The waiting line (queuing) theory is not a topic of this text. It is rather a part of the theory of probability and statistics. Note only that waiting lines simulation is one on the principal applications of discrete event simulation. Packages like SIMUL8, STELLA, ProModel, ARENA and similar, are used to simulate mass-service systems with waiting lines, and manufacturing systems where waiting lines are formed.

While simulating waiting lines, the most important parameters that we must provide are the distributions, expected values and standard deviations of service times and inter-arrival time for incoming clients or other elements. Remember that the **inter-arrival interval for the Poisson input process does not obey the Poisson distribution**. It has the exponential distribution.

Example: Manufacturing Simulation (BLUESSS)

Recall that BLUESSS is a general-purpose simulation system for C++Builder users. QMGW is a program generator for queuing models. QMGW was originally created to simulate mass service systems, mainly queuing models. As it contains some elements of the manufacturing systems like assembly operation and conveyor, it can be used for manufacturing systems simulation. Models with up to 800 blocks (servers, queues, assembly, etc.) have been successfully simulated. The actual version of the QMGW module permits up to 1000 blocks per model.

The new feature shown here is the capability of the assembly block to change its parameters according to the type of product being assembled. This feature can be useful while simulating flexible manufacturing systems. The QMGW assembly block simulates an assembly operation. It must have at least two inputs. The parts are taken from the inputs and assembled. This operation consists in creating a new part from the necessary components. Consequently, the parts that enter the block disappear from the model and a new part appears. The new part inherits most of the attributes from the main part (arriving at the uppermost assembly input). Server, assembly operation, generator and terminal point can perform any user-defined operations on the attributes of the processed part. These operations are coded by the user in C++. The QMGW assembly block has the following parameters:

Number of inputs
Numbers of parts to assemble at each input
Assemble time distribution
Additional delay at the output

The assembly operation can be executed only if at each input the necessary number of parts (components to assemble) are available in the corresponding buffers. However, in many practical applications these numbers may depend on what is actually assembled. For example, if there are two types of motors assembled, and may need four and the other six pistons. In the new version of QMGW, this number can change according to the motor type stored in an attribute of the part (e.g. motor block) that arrives at the input number one). The assembly time (random or deterministic) can also depend on the motor type. These properties of the assembly block make it a flexible and util QMGW component.

Consider the following simple model of a manufacturing system (Fig.1).

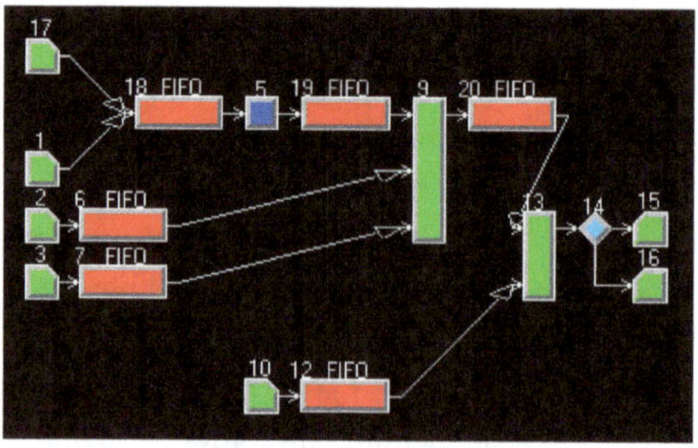

Figure 1. A manufacturing model example.

The product is assembled in two assembly operations shown as blocks no.9 and 13. The parts to assemble come from five sources (QMGW generators) no. 17,1,2,3 and 10. The generators 17 and 1 provide parts of type 1 and 2, respectively.

The GPSS-like final statistics are shown below. These are results averaged over 200 simulation runs. The complete specifications of the model blocks are given at the end of this topic. We will not discuss the results in detail. The final statistics show the queue statistics, like the average waiting time, maximal and minimal length and average length. The "lost" column shows eventual lost entities. The entity can be lost if it cannot enter the following block and there is no buffer to wait in. In our case there are no lost entities. Note, for example, the short waiting time for queue 7. This queue is not short, but it provides entities from the fast generator no.3. The parts do not wait long time in this queue, because the assembly block 9 needs several (5 or 7) parts and empties frequently the buffer.

Final Statistics:

Final time = 480.00

QUEUES:	Av waiting time	Lmax	Lmin	Av length	Lost
QUEUE6 :	12.536	123	0	23.598	0.00
QUEUE7 :	0.612	102	0	7.812	0.00
QUEUE12 :	1.064	58	0	7.051	0.00
QUEUE18 :	3.652	27	0	1.622	0.00
QUEUE19 :	69.860	101	0	30.357	0.00
QUEUE20 :	35.725	43	0	11.093	0.00

SERVERS:	Service time	Idle time	Idle %	Lost	Served
SERV5 :	359.163	120.837	25.17	0.00	210.70
ASSEMBL.:	Service time	Idle time	Idle %	Lost	Served
ASSE9 :	345.328	134.672	28.06	0.00	150.61
ASSE13 :	389.145	90.856	18.93	0.00	126.53

TERMINAL: Count(average)

TERM15: 43.93

TERM16: 82.58

TOTAL Terminal output = 126.51

Total cost = 1927.83

Average time in system = 14.19

The following image shows the confidence intervals for the length of the queue 7. The yellow line is the average queue length and the other two lines show the upper and lower limit of the confidence interval. In other words, the queue length is between the two limits with probability 0.9. This figure shows how little informative is the average value of this variable. Note that this analysis is dynamic and the results are shown as functions of time.

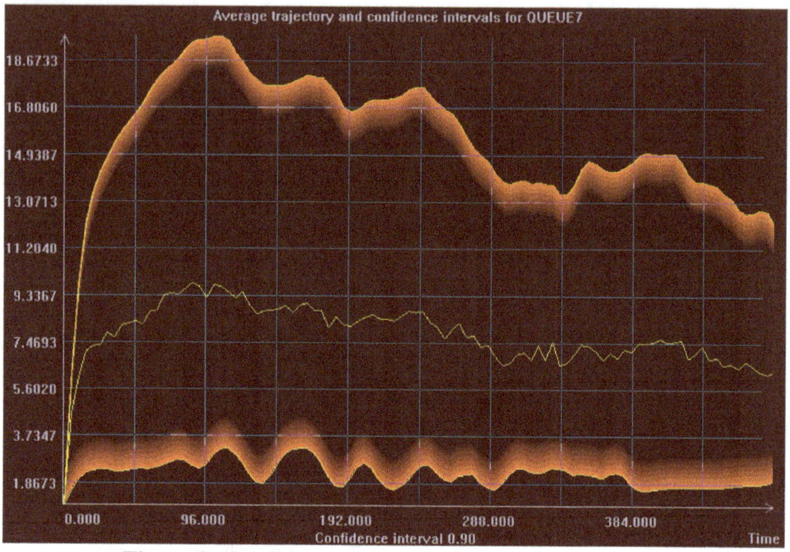

Figure 2. Confidence intervals for waiting line nr.7.

Chapter 5

General Purpose Software Tools

BLUESSS

General features

Blues Simulation System (BLUESSS) evolved from the PASION and PSM++ packages, related to Delphi. Some applications and remarks on discrete event simulation can be found in Raczynski (2000),(2004),(2006)
.

BLUESSS is a simulation language and has the BLUESSS-to-C++ translator. So, the user can code his model, or use one of the BLUESS modules to create models without coding. However, direct coding in BLUESSS language may be more flexible, in particular for object- and agent-based models.

The following modules (source code generators) are included in the BLUESSS package:

* Queuing Model Generator
* Flow diagrams. Continuous simulation using signal flow diagrams.
* Continuous simulation using bond graphs.
* Continuous simulation, ordinary differential equations.

While using the above modules, the BLUESS system generates the source BLUESSS code, translates into C++ and invokes the C++Builder which produces the executable program. The event queue in BLUESSS works due to the three-phase discrete simulation strategy O'Keefe (1986).

Using the QMG module the user defines the model in the Arena-like style, with no coding at all. As the process of creating exe file (stand-alone, independent executable) passes through the C++ compilation, BLUESSS QMG module can use all the features of C++ (see figure 1).

In other words, the comparison of QMG with, for example, Arena can be summarized in the following table:

Use Arena:	Why not replace it with:
Create model flowchart with Arena	Use QMG graphical model editor
Learn SIMAN, learn Arena manual including 30 pages of entity attribute and expression specifications, code the necessary expressions	Use C++

Table 1. Creating intelligent objects (Arena vs. BLUESSS)

Note that the QMG graphical model editor is very simple and can be dominated in 15 minutes of "training," even without consulting any documentation.

The objects created in QMG can be equipped with simple abilities (logical expressions, additional attributes) or with any complicated decision making algorithms, like fuzzy logic, iterative optimization algorithms, neural nets, database consulting. They can execute external programs or use external files. The object can do everything that can be coded in C++. There are no restrictions on the type and size of its attributes (those can be numbers, strings, arrays, pointers, and/or C++ structures of any kind). If required, the object can communicate through Internet, sing a song, display an OpenGL image, execute an external program, etc. There are some restrictions on the use of pointers. When the object disappears, it must execute a user-provided code to free the memory allocated to the pointed structures. Otherwise, memory leaks can occur.

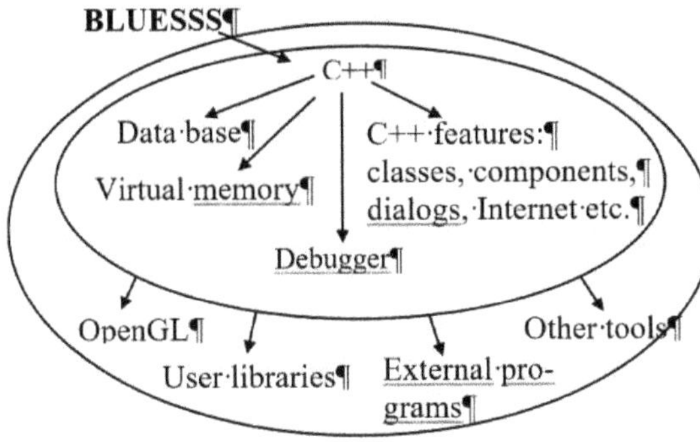

Figure 1. Bluesss features.

Scheduled and conditional events

Anywhere inside the event code or in the *Start* (main) program segment, an event can be scheduled for execution. For example, the statement

```
schedule client[4]->arrives to TIME + Negexp(2.5);
```

schedules the event arrives of object number 4 of process client to be executed at time instant equal to the current model TIME plus a random interval with exponential distribution, expected value 2.5,

Conditional events are not explicitly scheduled. They are executed when a given logical condition changes from false into true. So, the execution of such events can be related to the state of the model. In such case the event becomes a “state event” (state and conditional events are synonyms in the following). As these events are almost always related to the model state, the execution of such event can occur only if any other model event is executed because then the model state can change.

The header of a conditional event contains the event name and the name of the condition, separated by commas. For example, the following event event:

```
event myevent,somecond;
outlne(cnv,clWhite, “Condition somecond” +FloatToStr(TIME));
endev;
```

will be executed when the event “somecond” becomes true. Both "myevent" and "somecond" are user-defined identifiers. You can use as many conditional events and conditions as you want. The condition names must be unique in the whole program. The event myevent simply displays on the screen the comment "Conditions somecond xxx," where xxx is the value of the current model time.

If you use conditional events, you must define the corresponding conditions. This can be done anywhere in the body of any model event. However, the definition of the condition should appear in an event that is executed frequently, for example an event which integrates the state of a continuous process, or in a permanently active event. For example, if x[2] is a state vector component of a continuous process, the definition may be as follows.

somecond=x[2]<-0.1;

According to the above code, the event myevent will be executed each time when x[2] becomes less than -0.1.

In a queuing model you can use, for example a condition

somecond=TIME>12 && nr(queue7)>10;

With the above condition, the event will be executed when the model time is greater than 12 and the length of queue7 becomes greater than 10. Remember that the execution occurs when this condition changes from false into true.

BLUESSS Code: Simple Program

Let start with the following example of a complete Bluesss program.

```
Person *a,*b;
// a and b are references to the two objects created in the
// start section

process Person,2; // A person. Two object can be genrated.
String name; // person's name

event one;
outlne(cnv,clBlack, "TIME = "+FloatToStr(TIME)+" Active
object:" +name);
if(TIME>2000){outlne(cnv,clBlack, "Click to terminate");
zaczek(); exit(0);}
```

```
if(thisobject==a)schedule b->one to TIME+1;
else schedule a->one to TIME+1;
// the above instruction meands: if I am a then schedule the event
// one of b, else schedule event one of a
endev;

start 1,2000; // one repetition of the simulation.
// 2000 is the final model time
czys(cnv,255,255,255); // this clears the screen
newpr a; newpr b; // two objects of type Person are created
a->name="Fred"; b->name="Jimmy"; // define the names
schedule a->one to TIME;
// Event one of object a (Fred) is scheduled. Jimmy waits.
$
```

In the above program, *outlne* is a procedure provided in the Bluesss environment. It displays a line of text on the screen (the next line), starting with line 1. When the limit of the actual window is reached, then the window is cleared and the line counter starts with 1. The *cnv* variable is the default handle of the canvas of the active window. Procedure *zaczek* is a program pause (it waits for a mouse click or a key-press. You can create the program using any text editor that produces ASCII text. The best way to do this, is to use your C++ program editor. Remember that Bluesss is case-sensitive.

The above code is a complete Bluesss program. The declaration in the first line introduces two reference variables *a* and *b* that will be used as pointers to two objects created in the main program section. Then, a process declaration follows. The process type is *Person* and the two objects of this type can be generated to run concurrently. There is only one event (named one) declared inside the process. With the *outlne* instruction each object reports itself on the screen as active one. Note that the attribute name is used to identify the object that issues the message. The instruction schedule **b->one to TIME+1** schedules the event one of the object B to be executed at actual time plus one. Observe that the *if..else* instruction means: "If I am *a* then let *b* become active within one time unit, otherwise let *a* activate within one time unit." This means that the two objects *a* and *b* activate each other.

The program will produce the following sequence of messages

Time= xxxx Active object: FRED
Time= xxxx Active object: JIMMY
Time= xxxx Active object: FRED
Time= xxxx Active object: JIMMY
Time= xxxx Active object: FRED
Time= xxxx Active object: JIMMY
......etc.

where xxxx is the current model time. The simulation terminates when the value of the model time reaches 2000.

BLUESSS Code Example: Cats

This is an example of inheritance and multiple object model. It can be used to check the virtual memory management on your computer and the speed of the Bluesss event queue mechanism. Three processes are defined in the model: A *CAT* , *HE*, and *SHE*. A *CAT* includes the following events: to hunt, to eat, to sleep and to die. *HE* is a male cat, he inherits all the properties of' *CAT*, but can also fight with other cats. As the result of this event, one of them may die. The process *SHE* is a female cat, she inherits all the properties from *CAT*, but she can have several little cats in certain time intervals. In the main program only one object is generated, of type *SHE*. After some time, *SHE* has little cats, they start with their own activities, and the population grows. Note that even with several thousands of cats (some tens of thousands of events in the event queue) the program slow-down is not significative. The program speed is limited rather by the text display procedure.

```
int idk;

process CAT,1;
String NAME;

functions
```

void CAT::kotek(){} // this is not used. Here you can insert you customized C++ functions for CAT

```
endfunctions

event HUNTS;
outlne(cnv,clBlack,"%T   ="+FloatToStrF(TIME,ffGeneral,7,7)+
"Cat" +NAME+ "hunts.");
if(Frandom()>0.2)schedule EATS to TIME+Negexp(0.1); endev;

event EATS;
Application->ProcessMessages();
if(xf0==char(27))exit(0);
if(xf0==char(32))zaczek();
xf0='?';
outlne(cnv,clBlack,"%T   ="+FloatToStrF(TIME,ffGeneral,7,7)+
"Cat" +NAME+ "eats.");
schedule SLEEPS to TIME+Negexp(0.1); endev;

event SLEEPS;
outlne(cnv,clBlack,"%T   ="+FloatToStrF(TIME,ffGeneral,7,7)+
"Cat"+NAME+ "sleeps.");
schedule HUTS to TIME +35+Negexp(15.0); endev;

event DIES;
outlne(cnv,clBlack,"%T   ="+FloatToStrF(TIME,ffGeneral,7,7)+
"Cat"+NAME+ "dies.");
kill thisobject; endev;

process CAT/HE,50000;

functions
void HE::kocur()
{}
endfunctions
```

```
event FIGHTS;
int n;
find HE n iff n!=INDX; if(n<0)return;
outlne(cnv,clBlack,"%T  ="+FloatToStrF(TIME,ffGeneral,7,7)+
"Cat"+NAME+
"fights with cat"+HE[n]->NAME);
schedule FIGHTS to TIME+Negexp(12.0);
if(Frandom()>0.2)return;
if(Frandom()>0.5)schedule DIES to TIME; else schedule HE[n]-
>DIES to TIME;
endev;

process CAT/SHE,50000;

event CATS;
int k,j,a,b;
j=random(3)+3; outlne(cnv,clBlack,"%T="+FloatToStrF(TIME,
ffGeneral,7,7)+ "Cat" +NAME+
"has" +IntToStr(j)+ "little cats.");
for(k=0;k idk++;
if(Frandom()>0.5){
newpr pHE;
schedule pHE->HUNTS to TIME+Negexp(100.0);
schedule pHE->DIES to TIME+Negexp(5000.0);
schedule pHE->FIGHTS to TIME+Negexp(200.0);
pHE->NAME=IntToStr(idk);
}else{
newpr pSHE;
schedule pSHE->HUNTS to TIME+Negexp(100.0);
schedule pSHE->DIES to TIME+Negexp(5000.0);
schedule pSHE->CATS to TIME+Negexp(1000.0);
pSHE->NAME=IntToStr(idk);
}
}
```

```
outlne(cnv,clBlack, "%Number of cats = "+IntToStr(NHE+NSH
E));
    schedule CATS to TIME+Negexp(300.0); endev;

    start 1,100000.0;
    randomize();
    Application->ProcessMessages();
    czys(cnv,250,250,250);
    pisak(cnv,0,100,clSkyBlue,clBlack,
    "Press space bar to pause/resume Esc key to terminate.,"
    "Click to continue," "","",""); zaczek();
    czys(cnv,250,250,250);
    idk=1; xf0='?';
    newpr pSHE;
    schedule pSHE->HUNTS to TIME+100.0;
    schedule pSHE->DIES to TIME+Negexp(12000.0);
    schedule pSHE->CATS to TIME+Negexp(100.0);
    pSHE->NAME=IntToStr(idk);
    $
```

As the result, each cat reports on the display screen each event that it executes, and the corresponding time value.

Using QMG queuing module

This module is used mainly to simulate mass-service, and manufacturing systems with waiting lines. In order to create a QMG flowchart, the user picks up blocks (like GPSS facilities or Arena modules), and defines the basic block parameters like inter-arrival times, service times, etc. Then, the simulation can be invoked. The entities (dynamic objects) appear, go through the blocks and disappear. As stated before, the additional entity attributes can be declared, being of any available C++ type.

The relation between the entities and C++ entity related code is very simple. Any entity which enters to any of the model blocks simply calls a global C++ function named SVOP. Both calling entity and block identifiers, as well as all entity attributes are passed to SVOP as actual parameters. For the assembly operation SVOP is called by each entering entity and for the new (assembled) one. So, in the SVOP body the user can identify the block/entity pair and code any required action. For example, entities can enable or disable model blocks (using the semaphore logic variables) or execute more complicated actions (figure 2.).

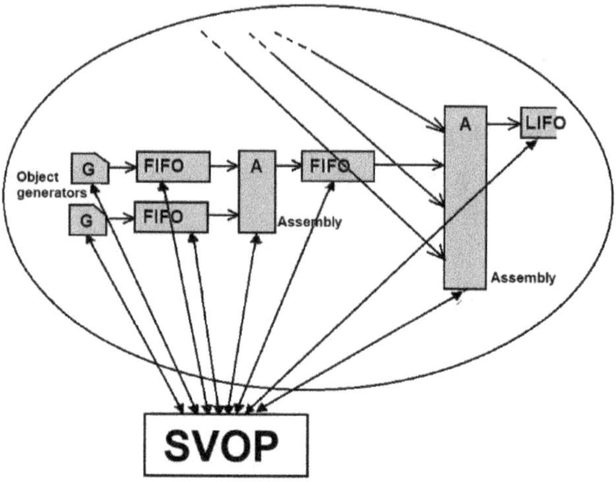

Figure 2. Fragment of a QMG model. Automatic calls to the SVOP function.

Suppose, for example that we need the following actions to be taken:

* If an entity enters the queue 59, its string attribute myname includes the string "dog" and the entity age is greater than 100 model time units (the time spent in the system), then invoke external program other.exe.
* If any entity enters the assembly block 42 and the sum S of the length of queue 39 and queue 41 exceeds 24, close (disable) generators 29 and 40. If S is less or equal to 24, then enable these generators.
* If any entity waits in any queue for more than 20 time units, display a warning message

In the below code n is the calling block number, SOURCE is the number of block where the entity has been created. TIMIN is the model time instant when the entity has been created, TIMQ is the time the entity has been waiting in a queue (if it is actually waiting), and myname is an additional, use-defined entity attribute. TIME is a global variable representing the model time. The function nr returns the queue length.

QUEx is the reference to the queue block number x, and SEMx is a boolean variable (a semaphore) that enables (if true) or disables (false) the block number x. DisplayWorning is a user-define C++ function (may show something on the screen, emit a sound etc.).

The SVOP procedure in this case may be as follows:

```
void SVOP(int n, int SOURCE,
  float TIMIN, float TIMQ, String& myname)
{
bool b;
if(n==59 && AnsiPos("dog,"myname)>0
   && TIME-TIMIN>100)
   WinExec("other.exe,"1);
if(n==42){
  b=nr(QUE39)+nr(QUE41)>24;
  SEM29=b; SEM40=b;}
if(TIMQ>20)DisplayWarning();
}
```

This is a very simple example. Inside the SVOP function the user can insert any C++ code to define the entity behavior and/or block operations.

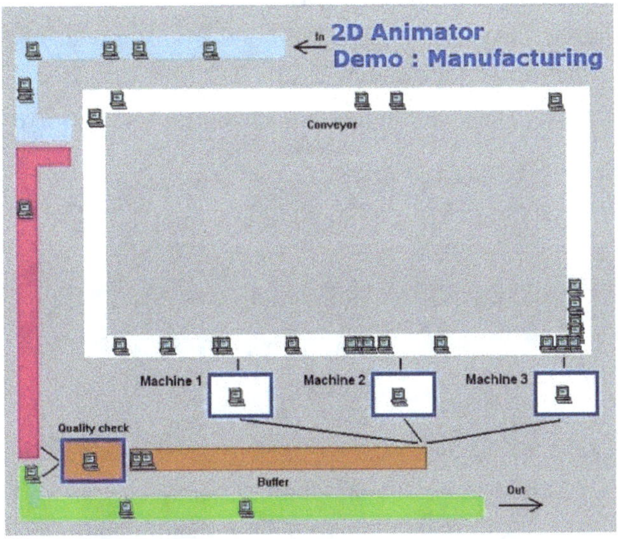

BLUESSS animation of a manufacturing system. Machines, waiting lines and conveyers.

More about BLUESSS

As stated before, BLUESSS is general purpose package. It contains several modules (source code generators) for queuing/manufacturing models, continuous simulation using ordinary differential equations, signal flow graphs, bond graphs or combined models. The user can create the source code or use any of the BLUESSS modules to avoid coding. Any BLUESSS simulation task passes through the source BLUESSS code, C++ code (generated automatically). The final product is an independent *exe* file, ready to run. The package structure is shown on figure 3. In BLUESSS everything (except the code taken from C++ libraries) passes through the BLUESSS source code and through the C++ code. The user can create his/her code or use the code generators. Other options are:

Queuing models: The queuing module generates the source code that is translated to C++ and compiled.

ODE (Ordinary Differential Equations) module receives the right-hand-sides of the equations. The rest is done automatically (source codes generation, compilation).

Block diagrams and signal flow module: The user defines graphically the model structure and the necessary parameters. The module generates the model equations, the rest is done as above.

Bond graphs: The user draws the bond graph model and gives its parameters. The rest is done automatically.

Animator: 2D off-line animation of queuing models is available (see figure 4).

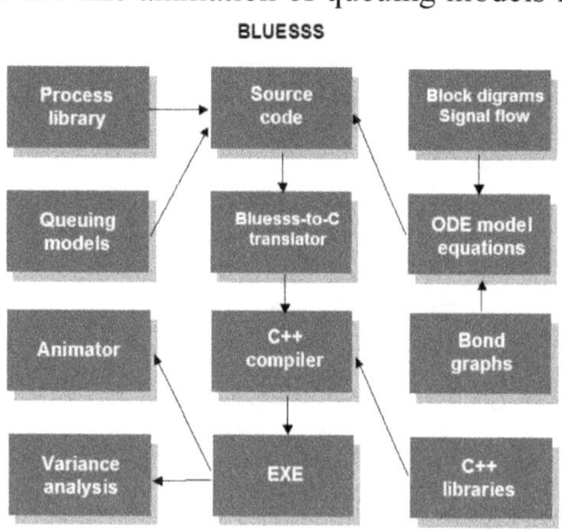

Figure 3. Bluesss package.

BLUESSS Variance Analysis

Variance analysis: postmortem additional statistical analysis can be invoked. This includes the max-min and confidence intervals for the model trajectories, shown as functions of time. This feature, provided by few simulation packages is very useful while simulating queuing and stochastic models. In figure 5, an example of such plot is shown. This is the length of a simulated queue. The gray region is where the length of the queue is supposed to belong with probability 0.92. The curve inside the region is the average queue length in function of model time. The average is taken over a series of repeating simulations. If the gray region is big (big variance), then it can be seen how little informative the average value is.

The user can see and modify both the BLUESSS and C++ codes. For queuing models, he/she can also use the SVOP functions as described earlier. Although the queuing models of BLUESSS are rather simple, the possibility of working on the generated code makes it possible to simulate any required object behavior.

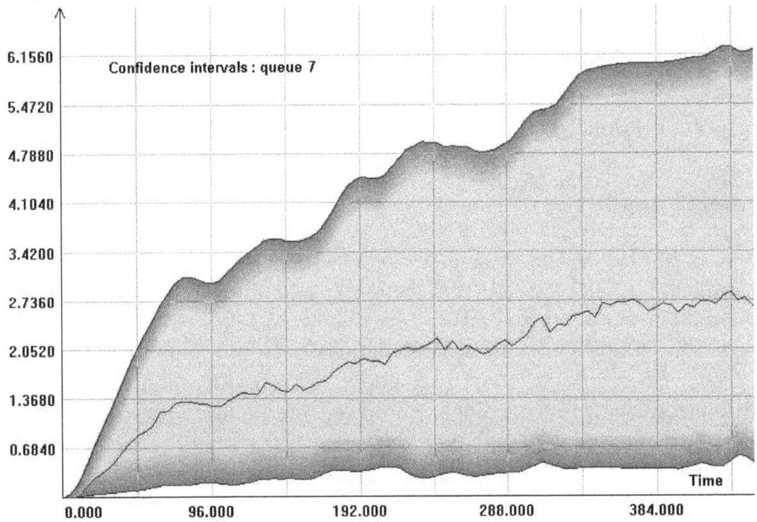

Figure 5. Confidence intervals for the length of a queue as function of time.

These are only some examples of BLUESSS features. BLUESSS can use any tools available in C++. Interesting animations, both for continuous and discrete event models can be created using the OpenGL graphics. Some tools that facilitate the BLUESSS-OpenGL communication are provided in the package.

Observe (figure 3) that both discrete event and continuous models result in the BLUESSS source code. The only difference is that the continuous models are simulated as a sequence of events with a small time step. Each event is a call to one of the possible numerical methods for ODE. This means that at the source code level the user can mix discrete and continuous models in the same simulation program.

BLUESSS is not a widely known or important commercial software. This is rather a proposal on a possible direction in simulation software development. The point is that what is really needed in discrete event simulation consists in the fast clock machine (event queue management) and good model structure definition tools.

The algorithmic aspect of the modeling, like intelligent object behavior, should be handled by a high level algorithmic language rather than complicated parameter specification and expression building incorporated in the package. Using one of already developed and powerful object-oriented language in the background gives us much more versatile tool to handle all that is not a simple queuing and discrete event simulation. Moreover, as we discuss professional level of simulation tasks, there are few users who don't already dominate C++ or similar tools.

References

O'Keefe R.M (1986) The three-phase approach: A comment on strategy-related characteristics of discrete event languages and models, SIMULATION 47(5), November 1986, pp. 208-210.

Raczynski S. (2000) Alternative mathematical tools for modeling and simulation: Metric space of models, Uncer-tainty, Differential Inclusions and Semi-discrete Events, Proceeedings, European Simulation Symposium ESS2000, Hamburg, Germany, September 2000 (Keynote plenary speach).

Raczynski S. (2004) Simulation of the Dynamic Interactions Between Terror and Anti-Terror Organizational Structures, The Journal of Artificial Societies and Social Simulation, vol.7, no.2, England, 2004.
http://jasss.soc.surrey.ac.uk/7/2/8.html

9. Raczynski S. (2006) Modeling and Simulation: Computer Science of Illusion, Wiley, England.

Basic, Fortran, Algol, C, Pascal, Siman and other programming languages

Do not use algorithmic languages such as BASIC, FORTAN, PASCAL or C to develop simulation programs. It would be a waste of your time. Use a simulation language or package appropriate for your problem.

CAD Motion

A full-featured, highly interactive modeling and simulation system specifically created for animating engineering drawings produced with AutoCAD. Features include full-function simulation accuracy end EMS support. CADmotion is a variant of PCModel.

Platform: IBM PC.

Contact: SimSoft, Inc., 1020 Fifield Street, Brookings, OR 97415.

CRISTAL BALL

Crystal Ball 2000 is an easy-to-use simulation program that helps you analyze the risks and uncertainties associated with your Microsoft Excel spreadsheet models. Most Excel users attempt to understand risk by creating best, worst, and most likely case versions of the same model. However, these scenarios only predict the range of outcomes, not the probability that they will occur. Crystal Ball adds probability and automates the 'what-if' process for you.

Because Crystal Ball is an add-in, you don't have to leave Excel to do forecasting and risk analysis. Plus, Crystal Ball will work with your already existing models, so you don't have to recreate all of your calculations from scratch.

As a fully integrated Excel add-in program with its own toolbar and menus, Crystal Ball picks up where spreadsheets end by letting you perform Monte Carlo analysis (a technique for simulating real-world situations involving elements of uncertainty). You define a range for each uncertain value in your spreadsheet, and Crystal Ball uses this information to quickly perform thousands of simulations.

Crystal Ball is powerful enough for advanced users, with features like

Latin Hypercube sampling, macro extensibility, and cumulative data table distributions.

The results are dynamically summarized in easy-to-understand forecast charts that show all the outcomes and the likelihood of each. Crystal Ball lets you complete your analysis sooner with less effort and lets you make better-informed decisions based on the true probability of specific outcomes.

Available from: Decisioneering, Inc.

1515 Arapahoe Street Suite 1311 Denver, CO 80202

Tel: 800.289.2550 (US) Tel: 303.534.1515 Fax: 303.534.4818

EXTEND

A fully integrated application for discrete event and continuous simulation. Combines a flexible, iconic modeling system with build-in language for extensibility. Features include hierarchy, animation, sensitivity analysis, object-oriented modeling, self-documenting and interrumptible processes.

EXTEND+Manufacturing combines all features of EXTEND with a specialized library of discrete event blocks. Designed for operations improvement, information processing, service industries, distribution systems, material handling and transportation systems.

Contact: Imagine That, Inc., 6830 Via del Oro, Suite 230, San Jose, CA 95119, USA.

FLAMES

Unlike fixed, monolithic simulations, FLAMES is a framework for composable simulations that can be reconfigured quickly to support almost any current or future modeling and simulation requirement imaginable. FLAMES is separate from and independent of application-specific software, such as models of real-world systems and custom interfaces to specific external systems. In a FLAMES-based simulation, the application-specific software resides in software components that plug into FLAMES using mature, well-defined interfaces.

As indicated on the FLAMES page (http://www.ternion.com/), FLAMES features are as follows.

Support for modeling almost any type of system (land, sea, air, space) at nearly any level of complexity.

Support for modeling human behavior and decision processes.

Support for scenarios with one player or thousands of players.

Ability to integrate models from legacy simulations.

Powerful, flexible database manager for storing, controlling, and sharing scenario data in a multi-user environment (no flat files).

Friendly, intuitive graphical user interface for editing ALL scenario data (no configuration or parameter files that must be edited by hand).

2D, plan-view displays using terrain contour maps or a map from almost any 2D image file

High-fidelity 3D visualization

Detailed terrain and cultural feature databases that are perfectly correlated with 3D visualization databases

Support for interacting with other simulations and simulators using both DIS and HLA; DIS and HLA interfaces are fully customizable

Support for complex parametric trades studies and Monte Carlo analysis simulation

Automatic checkpoint/restart capability to protect against hardware failure during long-running exercises

Special facilities that support high-performance virtual simulators

Support for direct interaction with real-world C4ISR systems and other live systems

Contact:

Ternion Corporation

2223 Drake Avenue

Huntsville, Alabama 35805, USA

FORESIGHT

This is an integrated set of tools that is used to graphically modeling and simulation. FORESIGHT is a system level tool to model and simulate hardware, software and person in the loop before expensive engineering begins. It supports multiple levels of abstraction including full functional, behavioral and performance models. Co-simulation of executable models on distributed workstations, configuration management, graphical user interfaces and automatic generation of C code.

Platform: PC.

Contact: LOG'IN, 4, Square du Chene Germain, 33510 CESSON-SAVIGNE, France.

MATLAB

MATLAB is a high-performance, interactive numeric computation and visualization environment that combines hundreds of advanced math and graphics functions with a high-level language. The open system architecture enables users to view the pre-packaged functions, customize these as needed, or add new functions. MATLAB toolboxes extend power of the package by providing leading-adge algorithms and functions developed for signal processing, control system design, neural networks, optimization, and other applications.

See also: SIMULINK.

Contact: The Math Works, Inc., 24 Prime Park Way, Natick, MA 01760.

Mode FRONTIER

modeFRONTIER® is a multi-objective optimization and design environment which combines a comprehensive process integration platform with sophisticated, state-of-the-art, optimization algorithms, and powerful post-processing capabilities.

Process Integration

Coupling different CAE tools to create a single, integrated, environment becomes a straight-forward task when carried with the user-friendly GUI in modeFRONTIER. The direct interfaces available for many of the most widely used commercial tools, such as MATLAB and EXCEL, as well as several CAD and engineering analysis programs make for seamless coupling. Even for the software for which no direct interface yet exists, modeFRONTIER's generic text file interface allows the user to create a process flow which includes all components of the CAE environment, even in-house tools.

Optimization

modeFRONTIER has a full library of algorithms for both single- and multi-objective optimization. When faced with a true multi-objective problem (i.e. one where the objectives are in conflict) the user can apply one of the multi-objective algorithms and treat all objectives separately; such cases result in a Trade-Off curve, or Pareto Frontier, of designs, any one of which could be considered an optimum.

Optimization Algorithms in modeFRONTIER:

MACK - Levenberg-Marquardt - Multi-Objective Partióle Swarm.

Lipschitz - Genetic Algorithms - Multi-Objective Simulated Annealing.

Simplex (MOGA-II and NSGA-II) - SQP (NLPQLP, MIPSQP, NBI-NLPQLP).

B-BFGS - ARMOGA - Multi-Objective Game Theory.

www.modefrontier.com

MODSIM III

MODSIM III is an environment for building advanced models. It generates readable C++ code. The user can access libraries written in C++. The system under study is described as a collection of interacting objects. Each object module describes the object behaviors, called methods. Inheritance allows new objects to be defined as a special case of one or more general classes. The MODSIM concepts are similar to those of SIMULA, BLUESSS and other object-oriented programming languages. The advantage of MODSIM is that it generates C code (Simula is based on Algol and BLUESSS generates C++ code).

MODSIM III provides libraries of objects that can be re-used while creating new models. There is a graphical model editor that allows to graphically put the object icons and add parameters through dialog boxes.

Platform: UNIX, PC

Contact: CACI Products Company, 3333 N Torrey Pines Ct, La Jolla, CA 92037, USA.

PROLOG

The PROLOG language is based on a restricted version of the First Order Predicate Calculus. PROLOG is known mainly as an artificial intelligence language. In recent years several authors proposed special extensions of PROLOG for simulation. A first realization of such a simulation language was T/TC-PROLOG (Futo I.,Szeredi J., A discrete simulation system based on artificial intelligence methods, in Discrete simulation and related fields, A. Javor ed., North Holland, Amsterdam.

Using PROLOG it is possible to perform special goal-oriented simulation, where the simulation is directed to find the appropriate activities and synchronization of processes to reach a predefined final state, the goal state.

Alain Colmerauer and his coworkers created the first version of Prolog in France at the University of Marseilles in the 1970's. Clocksin and Mellish, of the University of Edinburgh further developed prolog. Today, most prolog advocates consider their version of prolog a standard. At first prolog could only handle non-numeric information processing, but today prolog can do just about anything that's required. In the early 80's, American's were still slow to accept prolog; it wasn't regarded as practical and LISP was the established language for AI work. In the meantime, Europeans and the Japanese were becoming increasingly excited about the use of prolog for AI work. In 1986, Borland introduced Turbo Prolog as one of the first practical versions of prolog for IBM PCs. Turbo Prolog later became PDC Prolog and was refined and distributed by the Prolog Development Center.

A new version, Visual Prolog is a complete programming environment based on the Prolog programming language. It contains everything needed for building large-scale commercial applications: graphical development environment, compiler, linker and debugger. Visual Prolog is the successor of Turbo Prolog and PDC (Prolog Development Center) Prolog.

Visual Prolog includes a large library with bindings to a range of APIs: Including Windows GUI, ODBC/OCI databases and Internet (sockets, ftp, http, cgi, etc). The development environment is written entirely in Visual Prolog, and contains a number of Code Experts and graphical editors for dialogs, menus and toolbars. Visual Prolog is very well suited for expert systems, planning and other AI related problems.

Visual Prolog supports: Windows 3.x/95/98/NT/2000, OS/2 and some support for DOS, Linux and SCO UNIX

Prolog Development Center (PDC) was founded in 1984 with the development of a Prolog compiler - later to be known as Turbo Prolog, Contact: Prolog Development Center

568 14th Street
Atlanta GA 30318
Phone 1-800 762 2710
Fax 404 872 5243
Email: sales@pdcAtlanta.com

Consult also: Forgaty T.C., A prolog simulation for combustion control, SIMULATION 54(2), February 1990, pp. 101-109.

Closki, W.F., and Melish C.S., Programming in Prolog, Springer Verlag, New York 1984.

SIMPLE

It is fully object-oriented simulation software that was released commercially in 1992 by AESOP GmbH. It has been used in industry, government, and research institutions worldwide. SiMPLE++ offers application objects templates, hierarchy and inheritance, build-in language SimTALK and debugger, remote control, interfacing with ASCII, SQL, RPC and C.

For an example of application consult Levasseur G.A., Object-oriented modeling techniques with SiMPLE++: An example using a bakery's mixing area, Proceedings of the 1997 Summer Simulation Conference, The Society for Computer Simulation Int., Arlington VA, July 1997, pp. 348-355.

SIMULA67

Simula is one the first high-level object-oriented algorithmic languages. The language supports all object-oriented mechanisms like definitions of object classes, object creation and handling and the inheritance. It was created at the Norwegian Computing Center in the

1960th. The most known version is Simula67(see Dahl O., Nygaard B., Simula - an Algol-based simulation language, Communications of the ACM, no.9, pp.671-678).

As an algorithmic language, Simula can be used both in continuous and discrete-event simulations.

In the system library of Simula67 there is an object class Process, which includes a clock mechanism. If we use this class as a prefix to any new class definition, then the new class inherits all necessary mechanisms of model time and event queue handling.

Simula 67 is an extension of Algol 60. The basic concept of Simula is an object. It is a structure composed by attributes and instructions. Schematically, the object is represented as follows.

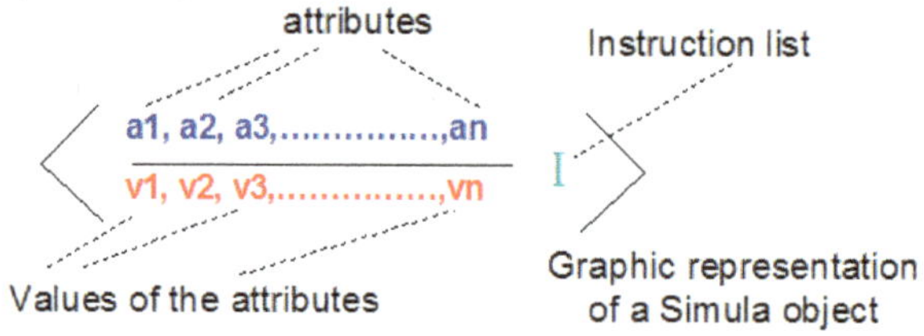

When created, the object executes the instruction from the list and then detaches itself, remaining inactive. For example, the following object may represent a point on a plane that can calculate its norm (a distance from the origin of the coordinate system). If we create an object of a class which inherits properties from the class Process , then the object executes its instruction list and deactivates itself. Then, any other object can activate it. The class Process provides tools for model time management, like the instructions hold (wait), passivate and activate . This gives us a great flexibility while implementing models of dynamic systems. The inheritance of properties makes it possible to re-use existent code to create new, more complex models. The attributes may be data or procedures. An example of and object:

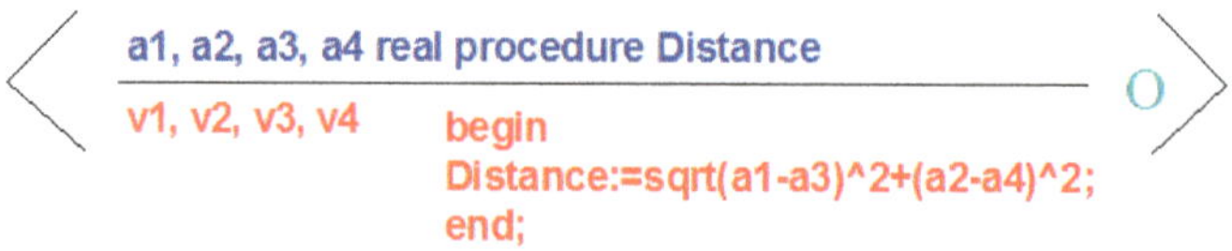

In this example the object consists in four real variables that represent the 2D coordinates of two points. The other attribute is a function which calculates the Euclidean distance between the two points. The instruction list is empty, which means that after being created, an object of this class does nothing and waits to be activated by another object.

The inheritance in Simula67 is realized by simple prefixed declarations. For example, Process class MyObject can be the heading of the producer class. If so, "MyObject" inherits all properties of a Simula process. This means that it can use the time-related instructions like hold and other mechanisms needed for dynamic modeling.

The objects of Simula are instances of the corresponding class definitions.

Simula67 was perhaps the first (and excellent) object-oriented language with simulation capabilities. After more than 50 years from its creation, it remains one of the most elegant and sophisticated object-oriented languages. The only disadvantage of Simula is its relation to Algol, which is not the most used and practical programming language.

Advantages of Simula:

The most complete high-level algorithmic language, object-oriented. Created nearly 20 years before C++, Delphi and similar tools appeared. An excellent simulation tool for models of any type. Recently, Simula is used mostly by researchers in the field of informatics.

Disadvantages:

Algol-based, difficult to learn. There are versions for PCs, but the user should be familiar with Algol to be able to use Simula. The process/event structure of the program is not sufficiently clear; certain experience in programming is necessary.

VRML : Virtual Reality Modeling Language

It is an ISO/IEC language developed by a combined effort of a group of companies and 3D designers and programmers for describing 3D scenes on the Web (fortunately from the beginning the effort converged to make it standard, no such luck with HTML until W3C was created). The documents have **.WRL* extensions that can be viewed by a browser with an appropriate plugin or helper-application.

This language is gaining more and more acceptance as a technology for displaying 3D graphics because it's a simple and accessible way to create interactive worlds. Also an important feature is that VRML is encoded in UTF-8 (Unikey) format, similar to your web page's HTML encoded in ASCII, so you can make very detailed 3D scenes using very small files that can be downloaded quickly - which is one of the main concerns when putting something on the internet. For example: you can make a 3D animation logo embedded on your home page that takes much less time to be downloaded than an usual animated gif.

See also: Virtual Reality

Chapter 6

Discrete Event Software Tools

In this section, you can find a list of, perhaps most relevant, software tools for discrete event simulation. Some of the packages are obsolete, they are listed for historical reasons.

ARENA

A package for discrete simulation with animation. The key is Application Solution Templates, specific modules that tailor the product to user specific needs. ARENA is built on the strengths of SIMAN, and CINEMA, combined with new concepts in object-oriented technology.

Platform: PC, DOS or OS/2, Windows, UNIX.

ARENA supports a great variety of model components (blocks). The user drags and drops the blocks into the model area, and then connects them with connection lines. The characteristic features are as follows:

The basic Process block has several options, like delay, size-delay, size-delay-release. If you select the most typical size-delay-release option, then the block works as a server with automatically associated queue. The other blocks are, among others: Create - to create a new entity that moves through the model blocks), Dispose - to delete an entity, Decision - to redirect the entity to more than one outputs, Batch - to group entering entities, Separate - to ungroup entities, and many others. The blocks encapsulate the main SIMAN blocks.

The attractive Arena feature is the on-line animation. The animation may be a simple animation directly on the model diagram, or the more sophisticated animation that can be seen outside the model diagram, but on the same model screen. The connections between blocks can also be animated. However, to make the animation more realistic, the connection animation should be disabled because the entities "jump" between block in model time interval of duration zero.

To make somewhat more sophisticated animations the user must use "stations" and "routes." A route is a path between two stations, and has a user-defined shape, length and speed. This feature might be difficult to learn for the beginner.

Contact: Systems Modeling Corporation, 504 Beaver Street Sewickley, PA 15143

BATCHES

A simulator for managing multi-product, recipe-driven batch and semi-continuous flow processes. It is data driven and modular in representation of the recipes. The graphical user interface facilitates data entry and analysis through case comparisons and animation. Helps optimize process configurations and operating procedures, equipment sizing and scheduling strategies.

Platform: SUN, Superstations, IBM RS/600

Contact: Batch Process Technologies, Inc., 1291 East Cumberland Avenue West Lafayette, IN 47906.

CINEMA

A graphical animation system. Used with SIMAN, it provides a user-friendly tool for visual analysis.

Platform: PC, SUN, DEC, IBM, HP workstations.

Contact: Systems Modeling Corporation, 504 Beaver Street Sewickley, PA 15143

CSL

The Control and Simulation Language was one of the first simulation languages, developed in the 50s. In fact, the name is somewhat confusing; the language has no capabilities for automatic control or similar tasks. It is a discrete simulation language that implements the Activity Scanning (AS) simulation strategy.

CSL is obsolete and not used recently. However, for historical reasons some CSL concepts are described here in more detail.

CSL is based on Fortran. Compared to Fortran, it has three new elements: the clock mechanism, entity class definition and sets of entities.

The clock mechanism manages a set of variables named time variables. These variables store various time instants. They are subject to the clock algorithm, and may be used in user-defined logical expressions. The time named CLOCK starts with value equal to zero. Then, all possible model activities are scanned, according to the following figure.

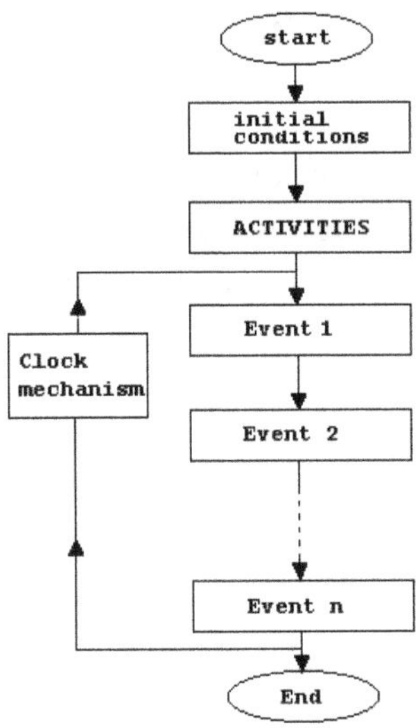

CSL program

The events are defined by the user and normally have the following structure.

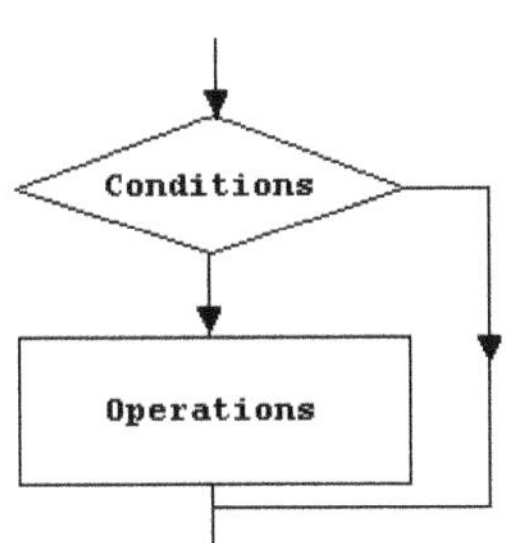

CSL event description

In the conditional part of the event the user should use one or more time variables. Moreover, the main condition should be TX EQ 0, where

TX is a time variable. So, only the events with corresponding time variables equal to zero will be executed. After terminating activity scanning, the CLOCK is set equal to the value of the nearest time variable greater than the CLOCK, this means to the time instant of next possible event. After this, all the time variables are being decreased by the same time interval. This way, in the next time, the next event(s) will be executed. The time variables can be declared by the user as global variables, or can be attached to model entities (each entity having its own time variable).

The following line is an example of a CSL class definition.

CLASS TIME CLIENT SET OUTSIDE, QUEUE, SERVICE

This defines a class named client (e.g. clients in a bank). The word TIME tells that each client has its own time variable. A client may belong to the sets OUTSIDE, QUEUE (waiting to be served) or SERVICE (being served). The reference T.CLIENT.K can be used to refer to the time variable of the client number K.

The program code includes only the initial part (initial conditions and the word ACTIVITIES), and then the event codes. The order the user puts the events in the program, is not relevant (except possible simultaneous events). The clock part is hidden and runs automatically. The code of an event should contain a conditional part and some operations. The operations are NOT executed if the conditions fail. For example, the arrivals of a client can be described as the following event code.

```
BEGIN
T.ARRIVAL EQ 0
T.ARRIVAL = NEGEXP(20)
FIND K OUTSIDE FIRST
CLIENT K FROM OUTSIDE
CLIENT K TAIL QUEUE
```

Note that this event reschedules itself to be executed after a random time interval (exponential distribution with mean equal to 20 time units). The main condition is T.ARRIVAL = 0, where T.ARRIVAL is a time variable. FIND finds a client being outside the bank. The client is taken from outside and put as the last one waiting in the queue. The instruction FIND returns also a logical value. If it fails (there are no clients outside), the following "operational" part of the event is not executed.

As mentioned above, this description of CSL is given here only for historical reasons. CSL is now obsolete and completely forgotten. However, some important simulation concepts were introduced in this language perhaps for the first time in the history of computer simulation.

FACTOR

This is an integrated software system, which provides a full range of capacity management applications including detailed finite capacity scheduling, accurate operations planning and engineering analysis. FACTOR/AIM uses graphical user interface, database and simulation technologies.

Contact: Pritsker Corporation, Suite 500, 8910 Purdue Road, Indianapolis, IN 46268-117, USA.

GIBBS

GIBBS is the Generalized Interaction Based Simulation Specification. It is a conceptual framework introduced through a description of its object classification scheme. The modeler views a manufacturing system as a collection of entities and interactions. An entity is a subsystem which changes its internal state in response to changes in its environment and/or the passage of time. Any subsystem at any level of abstraction maybe considered an entity. Examples include assembly lines, machine tools, controllers, fixtures, and parts. The GIBBS entities may be active, passive, static or dynamic. Static entities exist in the model throughout a period of interest, and the dynamic entities exist temporarily. The SPG (Simulation Program Generator) converts GIBBS model specification into an executable model. It initiates a master simulation object, instantiates objects within the GIBBS specification, defines their logical dependencies, and links these objects to the master simulation object to form a composite model.

Consult: GIBBS: A model specification framework for multi-stage, manufacturing system design. SIMULATION 56(6), June 1991, San Diego.

GPSS

A simulation language for discrete-event simulation, applied mainly to queuing models like mass service and manufacturing systems. First introduced in 1961. A GPSS model takes the form of block diagrams. There are more than 50 block types available, each of them having a name and graphical symbol. The main GPSS concept is a transaction. Transactions may be clients in a shop, cars on the street, parts to be processed, etc. The model defines the "life" of a transaction while passing through the GPSS blocks. For example, a simple one-queue-one-server model can be represented by the following diagram.

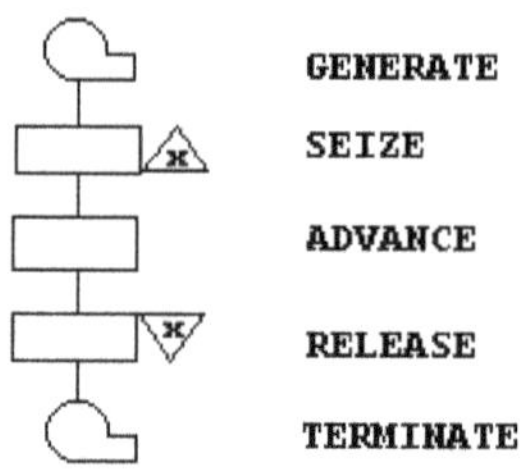

GENERATE block creates clients (transactions). The client occupies server x (SEIZE), then remains in the service for some time interval (ADVANCE), releases the server and disappears entering the TERMINATE block. If the server is occupied, a client that attempts to enter it waits in a queue.

After running the simulation, GPSS provides basic statistics like server occupation, idle time, max, minimum and average queue length, etc.

The following figure shows another example of a GPSS model. Now, there are five servers with corresponding queues. Arriving clients SELECT the queue with minimal length and the corresponding server. The result of the selection is stored in a half-word transaction attribute PH1.

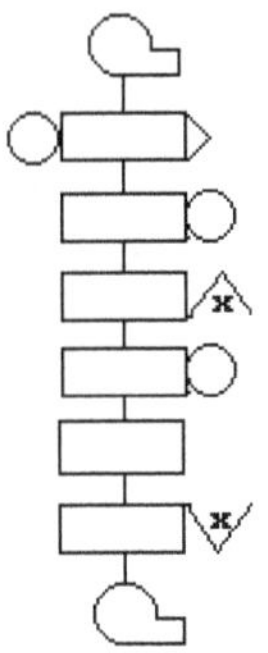

The corresponding GPSS code is shown below.

```
SIMULATE
GENERATE RVEXPO(1,0.2),,,,,1PH
SELECT MIN 1,1,5,,Q
QUEUE PH1
SEIZE PH1
DEPART PH1
ADVANCE 1.05,0.3
RELEASE PH1
TERMINATE 1
START 500
END
```

SIMULATE means the beginning of the simulation program. GENERATE generates clients with exponential time intervals between arrivals. The first parameter of GENERATE is the source of the random number stream (normally set to 1), and the second is the expected value for inter-arrival intervals. 1PH means that each client has one half-word attribute, referred to as PH1 in the following instructions. SELECT selects a queue and stores the result in the first attribute (PH1). The auxiliary word MIN means that it selects the queue (parameter Q) with minimal length. The second and third parameters define the range of queues (1-5). The QUEUE block is used to create statistics for the queue which number (index) is stored in PH1. SEIZE is the beginning of the service. DEPART tells GPSS that the client departs from the queue. ADVANCE is the service time. It has the uniform distribution with mean 1.05 and width 0.6

(+-0.3). RELEASE means the end of service (the server PH1 becomes free). TERMINATE terminates the client activities. START is the beginning of the simulation. The transaction counter is set to 500. Each execution of TERMINATE decreases this counter by one, so 500 clients are to be simulated.

Consult Gordon G., The application of GPSS to discrete system simulation, Prentice-Hall, 1975.

GSS

GSS is a user-friendly environment that supports model development, scenario development, discrete event simulation and analysis. GSS-MDG allows users to create and modify model structures on graphics terminal. It automatically catalogs the model structures for use in simulations. It allows the user to view model structures in a pictorial, hierarchical image, relieving the analyst of the complexities of managing large simulation models.

Platform: UNIX, AIX, RS/6000

Contact: PSI Simulation Systems Corp., 200 Atlantic Avenue, Manasquan, NJ 08736, USA,

or: Prediction Systems, Inc., 309 Morris Avenue, Suite G., Spring Lake, NJ 07762.

PCmodel

A highly interactive character-graphic, full-function discrete event simulation system oriented toward manufacturing problems. PCModel features exceptional performance (speed), dynamic user interaction, file I/O, real-time process interface, EMS support, and ability to interface to popular spreadsheet and database programs.

Platform: IBM PC.

Contact: SimSoft, Inc., 1020 Fifield Street, Brookings, OR 97415.

Petri Nets

Petri nets (PNs) is a graphical modeling tool, which has been widely used to model and evaluate concurrent and dynamic behavior of systems.

PNs were originally developed by Carl Petri in 1962 to model and analyze communication systems. In PNs there are four elements: *places* (represented by circles), *transitions* (represented by bars), directed *arcs*, and *tokens* (represented by dots). In simulation terminology, places are conditions, transitions are events and directed arcs connect places and transitions. A token in a place means that particular conditions hold, no token indicates it is false. The transition fires only when all input conditions are met. Is so, it removes a token from each input and deposits a token on each of its output places.

The following figure shows a queuing network and the corresponding Petri net. This is a simple model of a server with its input queue and a network that generates requests to be processed by the server. After processing a request, the server sends a response to the network.

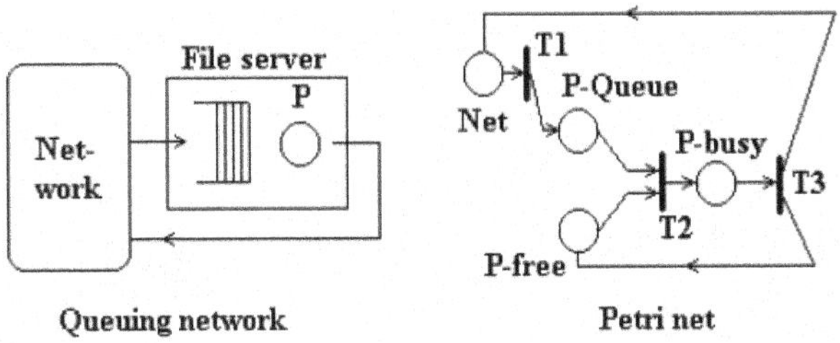

PROMODEL

This is a package designed for the simulation of all types of manufacturing systems. Completely menu-driven, its non-programming approach to modular, interactive model building coupled with colorful animation and a full package of analytical tools makes it quite useful.

Platform: PC WIndows

Contacto: ProModel corporation, 1875 S.State, Suite 3400, Orem UT 84058

QUEST

QUEST provides a flexible object-oriented environment to efficiently build, experiment and analyze discrete event simulation models. Includes extensive libraries of modeling and material handling system components. Data are dynamically represented in 3D models, icons and charts. Has built-in support for Just-in-Time (JIT) systems. Can communicate with spreadsheets and scheduling systems. Includes real-time model interaction and fly-through, as well as CAD translators and multi-person remote interaction.

Platform: PC Windows, UNIX.

Contact: Deneb, http://www.deneb.com

@Risk

@RISK performs risk analysis using Monte Carlo simulation to show you many possible outcomes in your Microsoft Excel spreadsheet—and tells you how likely they are to occur. This means you can judge which risks to take and which ones to avoid, allowing for the best decision making under uncertainty. With @RISK, you can answer questions like, "What is the probability of profit exceeding $10 million?" or "What are the chances of losing money on this venture?"

Sample applications:
Retirement planning
Currency valuation
Oil reserves estimation
Manufacturing quality control
New product analysis
Disease infection estimation
War games
Supply chain distribution

Contact: Palisade Corporation, 798 Cascadilla Street
Ithaca, NY 14850-3239
sales@palisade.com
800 432 RISK (US/Can)
+1 607 277 8000
+1 607 277 8001 fax

SIMAN

This is a high-level, general purpose system for discrete simulation. It provides for real time model execution and complete statistical analysis. SIMAN can combine continuous and discrete simulation, which gives the user the flexibility in the development of the model. Differential equations are solved in SIMAN using Runge-Kutta-Fehlberg algorithm.

Platform: PC, SUN, DEC, IBM, HP workstations.

Contact: Systems Modeling Corporation, 504 Beaver Street Sewickley, PA 15143

SIMFACTORY

SIMFACTORY is a part of the family of the products of CACI Company. It may be used to predict process performance. You graphically describe the factory under study through an easy-to-use interfase. Supports animation.

The other CACI products are: MODSIMIII, COMNETIII, SIMPROCESS, SIMSCRIPT, NETWORK II.5.

Platform: PC, workstation or host.

Contact: CACI Products Company, 3333 North Torrey Pines Court, La Jolla, California 92037.

SIMIO

The *Simio modeling software* lets you build and run dynamic 3D animated models of a wide range of systems - e.g. factories, supply chains, emergency departments, airports, and service systems. Simio employs an object approach to modeling, whereby models are built by combining objects that represent the physical components of the systems.

An object has its own custom behavior as defined by its internal model that responds to events in the system. For example, a production line model is built by placing objects that represent machines, conveyors, forklift trucks, aisles, etc. You can build your models using the objects provided in the Standard Object Library, which is general purpose set of objects, which comes standard with Simio. You can also build your own libraries of objects that are customized for specific application areas. As you see shortly you can also modify and extend the Standard Library object behavior using process logic.

In Simio object definition and model are the same thing. Whenever you build a model you have defined the logic for an object that can be used in other models. An object (or model) is defined by its properties, states, events, external view, and logic. These are key Simio concepts to understand for building and using objects.

Properties are input values that can be specified by the user of the object. For example, an object representing a server might have a property that specifies the service time. When the users places the server object into their facility model, they would also specify property value. An object's states are dynamic values that may change as the model executes. For example, the busy and idle status of a server object could be maintained by a state variable named Status that is changed by the object each time it starts or ends service on a customer. Events are things that the object may "fire" at selected times. For example, a server object might have an event fire each time the server completes processing of a customer, or a tank object might fire an event whenever it reaches full or empty. Events are useful for informing other objects that something important has happened.

The external view of an object is the 3D graphical representation of the object. This is what a user of the object will see when it is placed in their facility model.

The object's logic is an internal model that defines how the object responds to specific events that may occur. For example, a server object may have a model that specifies what actions take place when a customer arrives at the server. The internal model gives the object its unique behavior. One of the powerful features of Simio is that whenever you build a model of a system, you can turn that model into an object definition by simply adding some input properties and an external view. Your Introduction to Simio -2-model can then be placed as a sub-model within a higher-level model. Hence, hierarchical modeling is very natural in Simio.

Contact:
Simio LLC
504 Beaver Street
Sewickley, Pa 15143
www.simio.biz

SIMNET II

SIMNET II is a powerful discrete event simulation language developed by Dr. Hamdy A. Taha. Hamdy Taha is a Professor of Industrial Engineering at the University of Arkansas, Fayetteville.

SIMNET II is a network-based discrete event simulation language. Its design is based on the fact that the majority of discrete simulation systems are, in effect, queuing situations. SIMNET II uses four nodes to model a system: A source which generates entities, a queue in which entities wait, a facility where service is performed, and an auxilliary which functions as an infinite capacity facility.

Nodes in SIMNET II are connected by branches. As transactions flow across a branch, they invoke special functions through the use of special assignments. This capability differentiates SIMNET II from other discrete event simulation languages in that it does not require external subroutines to complete complex mathematical computations.

Simulation is a statistical experiment. SIMNET II provides, therefore, capabilities that account for the statistical peculiarities of the simulation experiment. These capabilities include the estimation of the transient period for a simulation run, and the collection of global statistical output based on the subinterval and the replication methods for both default and user-defined statistical variables. Mainframe, mini, and micro-computer versions of SIMNET II are available and all versions are fully compatible.

SIMNET II has been used extensively in a wide range of applications that included stock market analysis, reliability assessment, materials handling, transportation and logistics, inventory control, network analysis, and manufacturing. The design of the language is particularly well suited to modeling complex manufacturing systems such as job-shop scheduling and flexible manufacturing.

Platform: SIMNET II is available in mainframe and mini computer versions for UNIX operating systems and in a microcomputer version for IBM compatible PCs using DOS. SIMNET II has also been successfully ported to a PC platform running LINUX.

SIMNET and SIMNET II are registered trademarks of SimTec, Inc

Contact: SimTec, Inc.,

P.O. Box 3492

Fayetteville, AR 72702
Phone: (501) 756-6146
FAX: (501) 575-7446

SIMSCRIPT II

SIMSCRIPT II.5 is a powerful, free-form, English-like simulation language designed to greatly simplify writing programs for simulation modelling. Programs written in SIMSCRIPT II.5 are easily read and maintained. They are accurate, efficient, and generate results which are acceptable to users. Unlike other simulation programming languages, SIMSCRIPT II.5 requires no coding in other languages. SIMSCRIPT II.5 has been fully supported for over 33 years. Contributing to the wide acceptance and success of SIMSCRIPT II.5 modelling are:

DESIGN: A powerful world view, consisting of Entities and Processes, provides a natural conceptual framework with which to relate real objects to the model.

PROGRAMMING: SIMSCRIPT II.5 is a modern, free-form language with structured programming constructs and all the built-in facilities needed for model development. Model components can be programmed so they clearly reflect the organization and logic of the modeled system. The amount of program needed to model a system is typically 75% less than its FORTRAN or C counterpart.

DEBUGGER: A well-designed package of program debug facilities is provided. The required tools are available to detect errors in a complex computer program without resorting an error. Simulation status information is provided, and control is optionally transferred to a user program for additional analysis and output.

EVOLUTION: This structure allows the model to evolve easily and naturally from simple to detailed formulation as data becomes available. Many modifications, such as the choice of set disciplines and statistics are simply specified in the Preamble.

DOCUMENTATION: Because each model component is readable and self-contained, the model documentation is the model listing; it is never obsolete or inaccurate.

SIMUL8

Creating simulation software that is as simple as possible to use. It was achieved with the simple, but powerful use of "drag and drop to draw your business" and versatile dialog windows. Users can get started very quickly without a single line of code. In a few seconds an animated simulation can be running on the screen.

Simul8 has a number of alliances with other software companies that have complementary products and large installed user communities who can quickly make use of the value of simulation. A good example of this, is Visio business diagram customers who can build a simulation from a Visio diagram in SIMUL8 with one mouse click.

A link with AutoMod (3D realistic simulation) also exists for the more detailed analysis stage, once an initial layout of the facility is available and the specifics of material movement are important.

Through this alliance, AutoMod and SIMUL8 can address your simulation needs across the entire project, from initial concept validation to operating needs.

SIMUL8 is deeply integrated into Microsoft technology (OLE, compatibility with Office products and VBA).

SIMUL8 has ensured that even very new users can quickly create large and powerful simulations that match their business, y embedding template technology. SIMUL8 customers with expertise in specific areas embed this expertise into Wizard driven Templates that build SIMUL8 simulations automatically.

SIMCORE can help these customers to jointly develop these templates.

SIMUL8 Corporation
225 Franklin Street
26th Floor
Boston
MA 02110
Tel: 703 579 4073
Fax: 800 547 6389

SLAM II

This is a computer simulation language. SLAMII relies heavily on GASP and Q-GERT, combining them to provide in a single integrated framework. Developed by Pritsker and Associates, SLAM II is the most known version of SLAM.

SLAM II is an advanced FORTRAN based language that allows simulation models to be built based on three different worldviews. It provides network symbols for building graphical models that are easily translated into input statements for direct computer processing. It contains subprograms that support both discrete event and continuous model developments, and specifies the organizational structure for building such models. By combining networks, discrete event, and continuous modeling capabilities, SLAM II allows the systems analyst to develop models from a process-interaction, next-event, or activity-scanning perspective. The interfaces between the modeling approaches are explicitly defined to allow new conceptual views of systems to be explored.

Consult: Pritsker, Introduction to Simulation and SLAMII, John Wiley and Sons, 1984.

SMALLTALK

This is an object-oriented programming environment used to implement a tool for modeling and simulation of ecological systems. It makes it possible to easily represent individuals explicitly in the simulation, and to integrate the individual-based approach with a traditional population/concentration-based approach. The SMALLTALK objects are defined in classes object attributes (data) are called variables and object activities are defined as methods. As in other object-oriented languages, the general approach is to encapsulate data and corresponding methods. Instances are the actual objects belonging to a class. SMALLTALK programming tools are source-code browsers, debugger, editors and object inspector. The language was very popular in early 90s, and forgotten some years later. In fact, SMALLTALK does not offer any more than Simula67 developed 30 years earlier, and many other object-oriented languages.

STELLA

STELLA (short for Systems Thinking, Experimental Learning Laboratory with Animation; also marketed as iThink) is a visual programming language for system dynamics modeling introduced by Barry Richmond in 1985. The program, distributed by IEEE systems (formerly High Performance Systems) allows users to run models created as graphical representations of a system using four fundamental building blocks. STELLA has been used in academia as a teaching tool and has been used in a variety of research and business applications. The program has received positive reviews, being praised in particular for its ease of use and low cost

SWARM

The modeling formalism that Swarm adopts is a collection of independent agents interacting via discrete events. Within that framework, Swarm makes no assumptions about the particular sort of model being implemented. There are no domain specific requirements such as particular spatial environments, physical phenomena, agent representations, or interaction patterns. Swarm simulations have been written for such diverse areas as chemistry, economics, physics, anthropology, ecology, and political science.

The basic unit of a Swarm simulation is the agent. An agent is any actor in a system, any entity that can generate events that affect itself and other agents. Simulations consist of groups of many interacting agents. For example, an ecosystem simulation could consist of agents representing coyotes, rabbits, and carrots. In an economic simulation, agents could be companies, stockbrokers, shareholders, and a central bank. Simulation of discrete interactions between agents, stands in contrast to continuous system simulations, where simulated phenomena are quantities in a system of coupled equations.

Agents define the basic objects in the Swarm system, the simulated components. A schedule of discrete events on these objects defines a process occurring over time. In Swarm, individual actions take place at some specific time; time advances only by events scheduled at successive times. A schedule is a data structure that combines actions in the specific order in which they should execute. For example, the coyote/rabbit simulation could have three actions: "rabbits eat carrots," "rabbits hide from coyotes," and "coyotes eat rabbits." Each action is one discrete event: the schedule combines the three in a specific order, e.g. "each day, have the rabbits eat carrots, then they hide from the coyotes, then the coyotes try to eat the rabbits." The passage of time is modeled by the execution of the events in some sequence.

References:

http://www.santafe.edu/projects/swarm/overview/overview.html

MINAR, M., Burkhart, R., Langton, C., Askenazy, M. 1996, The Swarm Simulation System: A Toolkit for Building Multi-agent Simulations. Santa Fe Institute.

See also: Individual- and agent-based modeling

TAYLOR ED

TAYLOR ED is an object oriented simulation software for 2D/3D modeling

Taylor Enterprise Dynamics (Taylor ED) is an object-oriented software system used to model, simulate, visualize, and monitor dynamic-flow process activities and systems. Models can be displayed in 2D, 3D, or 3D virtual reality. With Taylor ED's open architecture, software users can access standard libraries of atoms to build models. Atoms are Taylor ED's smart objects and model building resources. In addition to Taylor ED's standard atom libraries, users can create new atoms themselves. Taylor ED's object-oriented architecture provides users with the ability to enhance and increase the functionality of the Taylor ED software system. It also provides simulation experts with a platform on which to create new simulation software programs for specific industries or for specific applications

Hardware Requirements: Pentium II processor or better

Software Requirements: Windows 98 or Windows NT

Provider: F&H Simulations, Inc.

info@bjalondon.com

VENSIM

Vensim is a software package for development of strategic business simulations and adopted by BRB Consulting as our core technology. It is an implementation of the concepts of System Dynamics. Vensim is developed by Ventana Systems Inc. and can be obtained direct from Ventana Systems or from Authorised Redistributors, such as BRB Consulting. See the Ventana Systems Web site for details.

Contact: Emma Bray
emma@brbconsulting.com

See also System Dynamics.

Index

www.ingramcontent.com/pod-product-compliance
Lightning Source LLC
LaVergne TN
LVHW050805220926
848485LV00014B/1458/J
* 9 7 8 1 6 8 0 5 3 3 8 3 5 *